GAMERS

LEVEL-03 - PART ONE

P. ANDREAS

ISBN: 9798323881758
Imprint: Independently published

CONTENTS

THANK YOU

As a teeny tiny pin, gazing up in awe at the huge haystack of amazingly talented writers, and their even huger haystack of awesome books, with heights reaching above the mountains, beyond the clouds, and into the stars, I can't help feeling small... smaller than small... smaller than the smalliest, smally, smallster, from the small town of smallton.

I would therefore like to take a moment to offer my hugest-of-huge thanks to all you literature-loving legends that have taken a moment in your lives to pick up and read my book.

So a thousand thank yous... times thank-you squared... to the power of infinity thank you... and with extra thank-you sprinkles!

REVIEW

Every word in this story was written for you, our Literature Loving Legends, and your feedback would truly mean the world.

Fabio and Zack are really eager to hear how they're doing, so... If you have a couple of minutes to spare, it would be awesomely awesome of extreme awesomeness, if you could leave a review on Amazon, or even pop one on Goodreads too!

If you only have a few seconds though, a quick-click rating on Amazon would be just as awesome!

Thank you so much.

01

THE NOT-A-KNOWN KNOCK

Sat at the dinner table, hunched over, and gazing blankly into his plate, as he pushed his food around mindlessly with his fork, was not just a troubled Fabio, or even a terribly troubled Fabio, nope... Sat before Mum, was a terribly troublesome troublingly troubled Fabio.

"Whatever is the matter my dear?" asked a deeply concerned Mum. "You seem ever-so troubled. I've never seen you like this before, and certainly not when you have one of your favourite meals in front of you, including your favourite side... a side serving of... absolutely **No Beans!**" she giggled, trying to encourage a little grin out of him.

"Sorry Mum," Fabio replied. "It's just that Zack and I were gaming online with Elle and Katsumi earlier, but then suddenly, all of a sudden, out of nowhere, by complete surprise, and without any warning at all... Elle just vanished offline! We've tried everything Mum... texting, messaging, video phone, emailing, social media, and even calling... but nothing. At this rate we may have to go old-school and write a letter, or use one of these strange machines we found online, called a fax, or a pager! And failing all that, we'll have to go even older-school and give some seriously serious consideration into sending a telegram by courier, using Morse code, or carrier pigeon, or lastly even... smoke signals! We're really worried Mum," he explained.

"Oh my," she gasped. "That *is* worrying my dear, and certainly explains your troublingly troubled looks. Let's hope it's nothing serious shall we, but whatever it is, we'll all pull together like we always do, and find a way to help," Mum said supportively. "And I have just the thing to tease out those terribly troublesome troublingly troubled troubles," and she sprang up from her seat and gave him a **HUUUUUGE** hug, gently patting his back.

"Hang on a second, that won't do at all," she said, as she suddenly stopped. "That's the upset Fabio hug, but what I need, is the... **UTR!**"

Mum paused for a moment as she flicked through the hug-for-every-occasion catalogue in her mind, until she found the **UTR**... the perfect hug for this occasion... The **Ultimate Troubles Remover!**

The Ultimate Troubles Remover hug is similar to a normal comforting hug, but the patting is replaced with... tickling!

Mum locked in the hug with one arm, and executed Ultimate Tickling power with her free hand. First she got a smile, then a chuckle, and then a few seconds later, out poured the laughs.

"Thanks Mum," Fabio giggled. "You always have the best hugs for every occasion," and he snuggled in for some more.

Just then, they heard three slow knocks on the door, each getting more seriously slow than the last.

Knock...

... Slow pause

Knock...

... Slower pause

Knock...

... Super seriously slow pause of extreme slowness!

They glanced at one another, with equally puzzled expressions. They know their knocks well, and that was not a knock they knew... that was a... **Not-a-Known Knock!**

Now Fabio and Mum know a lot about knocks,

Like a frantic Zack, with his *knock, knock, knock,*

Or his dad with his loud sharp

KNOCK! KNOCK! KNOCK!

But what was this, this strange slow knock?

This strange slow knock, was a Not-a-Known Knock!

If ever you are faced, with a Not-a-Known Knock,

You must take great care, you must never unlock,

To the window at once, to the

window you must rock,

And instead take a peek, to prevent any shock!

Fabio and Mum crept over to the window on the tippy-tips of their tippy-toes, with humorously over-exaggerated creeping actions, like a cartoon spy.

They gently moved the curtains a little, just the slightest of slivers, and peeped through to catch a glimpse of the owner of this strangely-slow Not-a-Known Knock. But when they saw who it was, they couldn't believe their eyes, and Fabio immediately dashed to the front door.

With his signature sock-slide across the hall, Fabio arrived at the front door in record time, but something was wrong... There was no frantic door handle wiggling, no fingers through the letterbox wriggling, and there were no beady eyes peeping through either. Yes indeed... something was very wrong.

Fabio quickly opened the door with Mum close behind him, and standing before them waaaaas... **Zack!** Arms dangling by his side, hunched over, and with his head hung low.

Fabio jumped over the doorstep, as Mum knelt down, and they both gave him a **HUUUUUGE** hug.

"Come on Zack my dear, let's get you inside so you don't catch a cold," said Mum lovingly, and they guided him in under their arms, and sat him down at the kitchen table.

"Have you eaten yet?" she asked. "We have plenty spare."

Zack shook his head. "Thank you, but I don't have the appetite at the moment."

"I understand Zack," said Mum. "I know another little boy that's been feeling just the same," she shared.

Zack looked up, and Fabio gave him a brave little smile, then grabbed his shoulder with a supporting squeeze.

"I know…. I'll make us all some lovely cups of comfort then," said Mum, with a warming smile, and she sent a quick secret text, then whisked up four large mugs of her famous hot cocoa, with mini marshmallows, chocolate sprinkles, chocolate sauce, and this time she even upgraded them with a towering spiral of whipped cream, and topped off with a cherry on top.

She served two 'not-too-hot ones' to the boys, who instantly took a sip, then licked their: chocolate foam, sprinkles, whipped cream, and sauce-covered lips.

She then served two hot ones for her and an empty seat…

"Who's the other one for?" asked Fabio and Zack in

unison, then immediately looked at each other with a grin and shouted "**SNAP!** you owe me a... erm... marshmallow!"

Just then there was a loud sharp ***KNOCK! KNOCK! KNOCK!*** at the door.

"Now that's certainly not a Not-a-Known Knock," said Fabio.

"No curtain peeking required this time," added Mum.

"Nope," agreed Fabio. "That's definitely... most certainly... Zack's dad's Knock!" he squealed, seeming in much better spirits.

Wow, my ultimate cups of comfort really are working a treat tonight, thought Mum, as she got up to answer the door.

She arrived back moments later with Zack's dad, who rubbed his hands together when he caught sight of his cocoa, and took a seat at the table.

They all cupped their hands around their drinks, dipped their heads into their mugs, and slurped a huge slurp.

Mum was the first to raise her head displaying a large whipped cream moustache, followed by Dad who had chocolate sprinkles all over his nose, which nearly made him sneeze. Next up was Fabio who was sporting a chocolate foam goatee from his top lip to his chin, and then... they all focused on Zack, who was somehow still slurping, as if he was going for the gold medal in the cocoa Olympics final event... the **SLURPATHON!**

After the longest slurp ever recorded in slurp history, Zack finally emerged from his cup of comfort as the super slurpathon gold medalist, and he also took first prize for the messiest face. He had a mini marshmallow and chocolate foam beard, chocolate sauce and sprinkles on his cheeks, and a whipped cream nose with the cherry on the tip! But above all that, the most important thing on Zack's face, was the huge **HUUUUUGE** smile.

They looked around the table at the massive mass of messy faces and couldn't hold back the laughter, and even Zack managed a few giggles.

Mission accomplished, thought Mum, as she handed them all a wet wipe to clean their faces, but Fabio and Zack refused to waste all that chocolaty goodness, so they scraped off and ate, as much as they could, before even considering a wipe.

"Well it sure looks like you enjoyed that," smiled Mum. "And I can see my cup-of-comfort magic has taken full effect. So Zaaaaack... my dear... Any chance you're ready to share your troublesome troubles with us, so we can all help?" she queried.

02

ASAP! ASAP! ASAP!

Zack looked at Mum's eagerly awaiting face... "I, erm... I think I'm ready now," he replied, with a little smile. "But the main problem is... I'm not sure there's anything *anyone* can do to help.

"Elle sent me a few texts, just before I came over. The first one was: 'Zack! It's an emergency! Yiayia has been rushed into hospital...'"

"Oh my goodness, that's terrible news," gasped Mum. "But please remind me, is Yiayia Elle's grandma?"

"Yes, that's right. Elle taught me that yiayia is the Greek word for grandma."

"Thanks Zack... and apologies, please continue."

"So... although I was in complete shock, I needed more information, so I texted back and asked if there was anything I could do to help... A little later she replied, explaining they were all at the hospital and she had an update.

"She explained Yiayia was stable, but she has a rare condition that requires a super special medical machine, and the big problem is... the hospital doesn't have one! And... the even bigger problem is... they don't even have the funds to buy one!"

"Wow, that *is* terrible news," said Dad. "But can I just clarify something first... Is this the Elle from Cyprus, that told you about the CataFarts tournament?"

"Sure is," replied Zack. "But *Daaaaad*, it's Cata**Karts**, not Cata**Farts**."

"Ahh yes, CataKarts... sorry Son," Dad corrected, clearing his throat with a few little embarrassing coughs. "And is this the same Elle that gave you her place in the tournament?" he continued.

"The one and only," confirmed Zack.

"The same tournament that ended up saving our house," Dad queried further, though of course he knew it was.

"Correct again Dad," Zack beamed.

"Then it's settled... we *are* helping Elle and Yiayia, and nothing will stand in our way!" Dad concluded.

"**Awesome!**" shouted Zack, jumping in the air.

Fabio quickly turned to his mum, with a pleading gaze. "What about us Mum?" he asked. "Are we going to help too?"

"I'm not sure my dear, I'll need to clarify something first too," replied Mum. "So *Zaaaaack*... If it wasn't for Elle, you and your dad, our best friends in the whole wide world, would have been forced to move away from us?"

"I'm afraid so," said Zack.

"Then it's settled... We're helping too!" said Mum.

"**Awesome!**" shouted Fabio, joining Zack with a few jumps in the air, but then all of a sudden they stopped, and sat back down with very serious expressions on their faces.

"This means..." Zack began.

"It's time..." Fabio added.

"For another..." Mum continued.

"**PERFECT PLAN!**" they all shouted, and stacked their hands in the middle of the table, then raised them up and cheered, "**WooHoo!**"

Just then, Fabio's phone beeped as a text popped through.

"Hi Fabio! You heard the news from Elle, bout the super special medical machine? x."

"Hey Katsumi! Yeah, we're gonna devise the perfect plan to help x."

"Oh Fabio, that's awesome news, I want to help too so please keep me posted x."

"Will do Katsumi x."

Fabio updated the gang, that Katsumi wants to help too, and they got straight down to business.

"Right then, who's the boss *this* time?" asked Zack.

"I reckon a grown up for this one," Fabio replied.

"I agree," said Dad, and they all looked at Mum...

"Challenge accepted!" she nodded. "And there's no time to lose, so we need to get this plan locked down **ASAP! ASAP! ASAP!**" giving a clap with each ASAP. "And the first order of business... is another round of drinks."

"I'm on it," Dad called out. "Two strong coffees and two warm milks coming up."

"Next, we need to find out the cost of this super special medical machine," she continued.

"Leave that one to me," said Zack, and he whipped out his phone to text Elle.

"Hey Elle, how you all doing?"

"Hi Zack, we're worried sick, but Yiayia is still stable... for now."

"Well Elle, hey that rhymes, we've been chatting about it here, and we want to help!"

"OMG, Zack! That's so kind, thank you all so much! I'm really hoping there's a way to fix this."

"There will be Elle, I promise. We *will* find a way, but for now, we just need to know how much that super special machine is."

"Erm... are you sitting down Zack?"

"I am now... Hit me!"

"Okay Zack, It's... 250... k!"

"K Elle, got it... two-fifty it is."

Zack relayed the amount to Fabio and the grown-ups. "Elle said the machine is two-fifty."

"Two-fifty? Fabio queried. "No problem, I'll just get my moneybox."

"No Fabio, as in two-hundred-and-fifty!" Zack corrected.

"Two-hundred-and-fifty?" said Mum. "I'm sure your dad and I can cover that."

"**Awesome!**" shouted Zack, and he updated Elle.

"Hi Elle, awesome news! Fabio's mum, and my dad,

can cover it!"

"I'm so sorry Zack, but the 'k' wasn't me saying 'okay', the machine is 250k, as in two-hundred-and-fifty-thousand!"

Zack's face suddenly dropped, and he froze.

"What's wrong Zack?" they all asked.

"Zack?" they probed again.

Zack shook his head, and out of his daze.

"Sorry guys, but I have some bad news. It's not just 250... it's 250k... as in two hundred and fifty thousand!" he explained.

First Fabio's face dropped and he froze, then Mum's face dropped and *she* froze, then Dad's face dropped, but how strange... he *didn't* freeze. He shook his head and fought his frightening freeze away.

"How come you're not frozen?" asked Zack.

"Because..." Dad began. "We've been down this road a few times now. It's a tough road and it's not been easy, but we've always fought, and in the end, we've always emerged **VICTORIOUS!**" he roared, unfreezing Fabio and Mum. "Now I won't lie... This challenge is a mammoth challenge, possibly our most mammoth yet, but you boys have taught me that it's still... just a challenge. Zack... tell Elle we're on it, and let's get planning!"

"Elle... we're in, we're going to find a way to raise the funds x," texted Zack.

"OMG times two Zack, that's amazing! I can't believe you'd do this for us. If I was there, I'd be giving you all the hugest hugs right now, and double huge hugs for you Zack! We're looking for ways to raise funds here, and Katsumi is trying to find a way to help too! Bye Zack x."

"Bye Elle x."

Zack got up and gave each of them a huge hug from Elle, then sat down and double-huge hugged himself.

"What's next Mum?" asked Fabio.

"Hmmm, let me do a quick calculation here," she pondered, rubbing her chin. "Erm, now **Z**... plus **F**... plus **GT**... equals **CC**, there we go, the winning formula! **Z +F+GT=CC**," she smiled, looking at three calculation-confused faces.

"Errr, Muuum," Fabio challenged. "What on earth do all those letters stand for?"

"Why, it's simple of course my dear," she replied. "Zack + Fabio + Gaming Tournaments = Completed

Challenges! So all we need to do, is find a 250k tournament."

"Lord Findington of Scrollville at your service Madam," said Zack, in a posh voice, as he got up and took a bow.

"Utterly splendid my dear," replied Mum, in an even posher voice.

"Anyone care to race me?" Zack challenged, as he grabbed his phone and held his finger aloft.

"Sure, why not," they all responded, as they scrambled for their devices.

"Ok then," said Zack. "But remember... I, am the master of the internet... So prepare for a **CRUSHING DEFEAT!**" and he counted down...

"**Three**...

"**Two**...

"**One**..."

03

GOOBADOOD!

Suddenly... even before he had the chance to shout GO! Zack's phone rudely interrupted him with a *Beep Beep Beep*, and an urgent email appeared in his inbox.

"**ABORT RACE! ABORT RACE!**" howled Zack. "I just got an urgent email, you all have to wait!" but the scroll challenge had already begun.

"Sorry Zack, no waiting," cried Fabio, frantically searching through the gaming sites, "You'll just have to try and catch up."

"Yeah Zack," Dad teased. "Maybe you won't win this one after all!"

Zack super-charged his finest whiny voice... "Buuut Daaaaad... that's not *faaaaair*," he protested, as he began reading the email. "Actually, forget that, phones down everyone... I've won!"

"How the... I mean... Awesome Zack!" Mum awkwardly grinned. "That must be a record; I only got to one website."

"Not sure how you did that buddy, but an 'Awesome Zack' from me too!" added Fabio. "I managed to scroll through five."

Now it was time for Dad to offer *his* congratulations, but instead... he ultra-charged *his* whiniest voice... "Buuut Zaaaaack... that's not faaaaair."

"Why, how far did *you* get Dad?"

"Erm... just to typing the 't' in tournament."

"The last 't' Dad?" Zack queried further. "I guess that's not *too* bad... for the one-finger-typing fumbler," he mocked.

"No," replied Dad embarrassingly. "I only got as far as typing the first 't'!"

"Oh dear Dad, you really do need to level-up your phone typing game," Zack joked some more. "I tell you what... when we have more time... how about Fabio and I train you up from the one-finger fumbler to the double-thumb-typing master, completely free of charge of course."

"Thanks Son, that's ever-so generous of you," Dad replied, with a super-sized serving of sarcasm. "Now, never mind me... what did you find?"

"Okay, do you want the good news first... or the bad?" asked Zack.

They all shouted their answers at the same time, firing a jumbled and noisy "**GOOBADOOD!**"

"Ahh, the old 'goobadood' I see," said Zack, as he quickly deciphered it as **good**, **bad**, and **good**. "In that case... Good wins!" he nodded. "And the reason I won so fast, was the urgent email. It's from 'Tourneys 'R' Us', the company that ran the CataKarts tournament. For my recent win, I've been invited to take part in a live, team-vs-team charity tournament... in Cyprus... and first place wins..." he paused for dramatic effect. "250k to donate to the charity of their choice!" he squealed. "And... they'll even pay for the flights and accommodation. All I have to do is find a team of five gamers."

"Zack that's not just good news, that's the tournament, the country, the funds, the flights, *and* the accommodation... that's quintuple-good news!" Mum cried with delight. "How is there possibly any bad news in that?"

"It's the flights and accommodation," he said in sorrow, as he looked down. "They're only for me and one grown-up, so how are you and Fabio going to manage?"

"Let's see the details first," said Mum. "So we know what we're up against," and she looked at the email.

While Mum was busy reading, the boys updated Elle and Katsumi.

"Awesome Zack! That's perfect! I heard about that tourney, but with everything going on here I never bothered to check. That prize can help Yiayia so you can count me in, and... I can't wait to meet you in person! x." Elle texted.

"Woohoo! What a fab find Fabio... I'm in! My folks wanted to help anyway so adding a week in Cyprus just sweetened the deal. And also... we're finally gonna get to meet! x." Katsumi replied.

In all the mayhem, Fabio and Zack hadn't even considered the fact that they would be meeting the girls in person, and their hearts began beating with a new emotion they had never felt before. It was a mixture of fear and excitement... It was...

Exfrightment!

After their exfrightment, the boys turned to face Mum, as she was taking far too long to read a little email.

At first she seemed frozen again, but then she suddenly reeled back in horrific horror, and shockingly surprising shock!

"**Mum!** What's wrong with your face?" Fabio fretted.

"Erm... Do you want the very, very, very, very, bad news, or the only very slightly good news?" she replied, still startled.

"The very, very, very, very, bad, this time please!" they all shouted.

"Well I'm afraid to say Zack, but this urgent email is not your first invitation... The reason it's titled '**URGENT**' is because it's the Final Reminder... The tournament starts on **Monday!**"

Fabio and Zack looked at each other, and inhaled until their lungs were maxed up to the max...

"**Aaaaaaaaaaaaaaaaaaaaaaaaaaaaaaaaaaaaaaaaaaaaaa aaaaaaaaaaaaaaaaaaaaaaaaaaaaaaaaa**," they screamed in panic until they ran out of breath, then inhaled again...

"**Aaaaaaaaaaaaaaaaaaaaaaaaaaaaaaaaaaaaaaaaaaaaa aaaaaaaaaaaaaaaaaaaaaaaaaaaaaaaaaa**."

"But how? How did I miss the first ones?" asked a puzzled and wheezing Zack.

"They went into your spam folder... look," pointed Mum.

"**SPAM**?! I thought all that annoying flashing and beeping was just an advert trying to sell me something," cried Zack.

"It's where your unwanted emails go," Dad explained. "But sometimes, ones you actually want get sent there too."

"I see," said Zack. "So although I'm the master of the internet, it appears I'm most certainly *not,* the master of spam..." he admitted.

"I knew this was all a bit too good to be true," said a frustrated Fabio. "No spinning blue rings of annoyingness, no internet emergencies, no full tournaments, but now we have the challenge of all challenges... Getting to Cyprus before the tournament starts on Monday, and... it's Saturday evening!!! We literally need to be on the plane this time tomorrow!"

"**Aaaaaaaaaaaaaaaaaaaaaaaaaaaaaaaaaaaaaaaaaaaaa**

aaaaaaaaaaaaaaaaaaaaaaaaaaaaaaaaaaaa," screamed Fabio and Zack again, with the addition of running around the kitchen table flailing their arms in the air.

"Right, then there's definitely no time to waste," said Mum. "**Code Red! Code Red!**" she called out in a military voice. "We need to upgrade to emergency speed... Ultimate Turbo Mode... Level-03!" and she grabbed her phone and began scrolling, almost as fast as Zack, as she looked up flights and accommodation for a week in Cyprus.

"Okay, no more shocks, freezes, frowny faces, or 'aaaaaaaahs' this time," she added, just a brief moment later. "But... I have some more bad news."

"Hang on a minute," said Zack. "You never gave us the only-very-slightly *good* news."

"Ah yes, well remembered Zack," said Mum. "The bad news is that the only-very-slightly good news is now more bad news!" she explained... to three puzzled faces. "You see... the only-very-slightly good news was that it's half term next week, so we don't have to worry about school. But... school holidays mean the flights and accommodation have... **TRIPLED!!!** I would have struggled with the standard prices, but there's no way we can afford triple."

They sat pondering for a moment, until Fabio broke the silence...

"So, we just need another tourney then, that's all," he said, unfazed. "One we can enter immediately, one that will cover the costs, and one we can win in time for tomorrow's flight, and... we need it **FAST!**"

"Say no more," said Zack, with a steely glare, and furrowed eyebrows, and he grabbed his phone. "This is the scroll challenge of all challenges. If I complete this, then I'll most certainly need a level up, but if I fail... then we won't be able to help Elle and Yiayia, so I'll be stripped of all my ranks!"

"Whoa, that sounds a bit harsh," said Fabio.

"Well, you know what they say... With great internet scrolling powers, comes great strippings of ranks."

"Erm, Zack... I've literally never-ever, ever-never, ever... heard *anyone,* say that saying! But, if they're your terms, then consider it done," Fabio complied. "Now, ready... set... **SCROLL!**"

04

WE NEED HOTAS!

Z ack did some swift scrolls up, then some speedy scrolls down, as his fingers began to blur. Next he was scrolling left, then scrolling right, as sweat formed on his head. He scrolled with his left eye closed, then his right eye closed, then scrolled with both eyes closed! He pressed the screen here, then there, then everywhere, then pressed using all his fingers and thumbs together. Finally, he spun his phone on the table, closed his eyes, pressed it one last time... and slid it over to Fabio.

"That's all my scroll power used up Fabio, I don't even have the energy left to look," said a drained Zack.

Fabio took a peek at the screen then dipped his head. "More bad news I'm afraid buddy... You didn't find a tourney."

"Impossible!" exclaimed Zack. "That can't possibly be possible," he continued. "I, Lord Findington of Scrollville, the master of the internet, always scroll and find whatever we need, no matter how difficult!"

"It's *'Earl'* Findington of Scrollville now," Fabio corrected. "**You've levelled up!**"

"But I don't understand," said Zack. "You just said I didn't find a tourney."

"You didn't... You found a... Competition!" Fabio cheered.

"Heeeeey, you can't scare me like that," Zack teased. "And also... is an Earl even above a Lord?" he asked.

"I'm not entirely sure," replied Fabio. "All this title business is very confusing, but it sounded like a cool promotion so that was good enough for me!"

"Then it's good enough for me too," agreed Zack.

"So just to confirm," added Mum. "Zack's found what we need, there'll be no strippings of ranks, and he's levelled up to Earl?"

"Correctamundo Mum," Fabio replied. "Now, back to the competition as it's about to get exciting... Firstly, it's not Player-Versus-Player, or PVP as us gamers call it, it's **PVE... Player-Versus-Environment!**"

"Interesting," said Zack, getting a little excited. "Tell me more!"

"Well..." Fabio began, taking a huge breath... "The competition is promoting that new flying game everyone's raving about called Wicked Wings, and you can win tickets, for any plane, to any destination, for you and one other person, and you get a bit of spending money while you're there too, and all you have to do is land the plane you need the tickets for, in the airport of your destination, and... and," and he ran out of breath.

"Well that doesn't sound too difficult," said Zack, seemingly unfazed by Fabio's latest word-splosion. "We just need to find the plane I'll be flying on, and the airport I'll be landing in."

"Erm, it's a teeny tiny bit harder than that I'm afraid," Fabio continued, taking another big breath. "You see... the level is set to the hardest difficulty, the wind speeds have been overridden to beyond maximum, it's *sooooo* foggy that you can't see the fog, as it's blocked by even more fog, and it's all happening during an insanely heavy, sleety snow storm made up of seven sleet and snow storms combined, and if all that wasn't difficult enough, it all happens at the pitchest black of the deadest of night, where the only light source is from random flashes of... of... lightning," he just managed to finish, though panting heavily.

"I see," said Zack. "That does sound a teeny tiny bit harder."

"Teeny tiny?" said Dad. "That sounds muchly much harder to me!"

"Yes, or even a lotty lot harder!" Mum added.

"Okay," Zack agreed. "So it's a muchly much, lotty lot harder! Now let's find that plane and destination!" and he began scrolling again.

"The smaller planes should be easier for us to land on those crazy settings Zack, so let's hope you're on a teeny one," said Fabio.

"Erm, the smaller the better, you say... Well I've found it, but it sounds a little bigger than small," said a concerned Zack.

"Why what's it called?" Fabio asked.

"The... Double-Quad Engine, Triple-decker, Super MegaLiner 854," Zack replied. "The world's largest passenger plane!"

"Hmmm... that does sound a little bigger than small," Fabio pondered, comically rubbing his chin. "Oh well, there's nothing we can do about that, so let's just hope the airport is equally huge then."

"Just found that too!" blurted Zack, after another speedy scroll. "I'll just bring up a few images," and he began prodding at the screen. "Hmmm, that's odd... All I can find are pictures of this small road with a little building next to it."

"That's no small road," said Dad. "That's the runway!"

"And that's no little building either," added Mum. "That's the airport!"

"Ok," began Fabio. "So just to clarify... In order to get the tickets we need, we have to land the largest plane, in the smallest airport, on quite possibly the most insane sounding difficulty I've ever heard?"

"Yep!" they all replied, fully expecting a well deserved whine.

"Okay then... Challenge accepted!" Fabio replied confidently, raising his hand for the highest of all high fives.

"**YEAH!** Let's **DO THIS!**" they all hollered.

Fabio and Zack texted the updates to the girls then sped upstairs, downloaded the Wicked Wings competition, and smiled with excitement as they began their new gaming challenge... In the vast cockpit of the ML854, and its zillion-trillion controls, buttons, levers, switches, and dials, across all the instruments, panels, screens, radars, and countless other tech! And to top it all off... their visibility through the windscreen was an extremely generous 0%.

Their excitement lasted a whopping two minutes, as they quickly failed over and over again, with their turns lasting mere seconds, as the horrific storm sent them spiralling out of control.

"It's no use," Fabio grumbled. "This controller doesn't have enough buttons... We need more buttons!"

"Then it's time," said Zack, and he dashed off to his house, and returned back moments later, with a small golden cardboard box, sealed in its original wrapping.

"Zack, you can't!" Fabio cried in horror. "If you open it, it will lose all its value."

"It's the only way," Zack replied, and they both winced as he broke the seal and opened the box, to reveal... his ultimate limited edition, shimmering golden coloured, elite pro controller."

They quickly set it up and got straight back into the

action, and this time their excitement lasted a whole... three minutes!

"Still not enough buttons!" said a now frustrated Fabio. "It has to be possible, we must be missing something."

Zack jumped on the internet, and using his speedy scroll powers once more, found out that you can use **TWO** controllers, so they immediately snatched up one each.

Fabio focused on the flight manoeuvres, while Zack's job was chief tweaker, for the zillion other controls.

"It's working!" cried Zack, as he tweaked away with perfect tweak timing, but Fabio was still struggling, and they were still failing.

"Zack, you're doing awesome," Fabio praised. "We have enough buttons now, but these little thumb sticks don't have enough precision."

"Then you need... **HOTAS!!!**" Zack cried out.

Just then Mum and Dad popped into Fabio's room. "How's it going?" they asked.

The boys turned to their parents..."**We need HOTAS!!!**" they yelled.

"HOTAS?" queried a puzzled Mum and Dad. "What's

this HOTAS business you speak of?" they asked.

"It stands for Hands On Throttle And Stick, like the ones they use in stunt jets." explained Zack. "We keep losing because we need more precision."

"One HOTAS coming up," said Dad, and he... ran out of the room, sped down the stairs, dashed through the door, and screeched off in the sports car.

Mum, Fabio, and Zack, stared at each other for a minute, confused as to what had just happened, then Mum scampered downstairs to catch a bit of 'off-duty' time, and the boys carried on practising while they waited for Dad to return from his strangely sudden disappearance.

They didn't have to wait long though, as a few more failed attempts later, they heard him screech back into the drive, dart through the door, scurry up the stairs, and burst back into the bedroom, sweating, panting, and doubled over, as he reached out and passed them a box.

"Wow, thanks Dad!" said a very amazed Zack. "How did you get one so late?"

"The... Mega... Massive... Monster... Store..." he replied, gasping for air between each word.

"Dad that's awesome, but there's just one problem," Zack pointed out. "You got the wrong one..."

05

GAMES, GAMES, GAMES, AND... GAMES

D ad looked crushed as he glanced at Zack, then Fabio, then Zack, then back to Fabio, then finally back to Zack. "But... but... all that speeding, and dashing, and screeching, and darting, and scurrying, and..."

"Gotcha!" Zack giggled. "Only joking," he laughed. "You actually got us one of the best ones. The... **HOTAS Ultimate Deluxo, Super Elite Pro XL5.2S v3!**"

Dad didn't have the energy to complain, he just glanced up at Zack, still panting, with a *'that-was-mean'* look on his face.

They hooked it up in an instant, with Fabio on the HOTAS and Zack on the pro controller, giving them the ultimate combo, or so they thought...

After many more failed attempts, the boys trundled downstairs in defeat, and plodded back to their parents, who were chattering away in the kitchen.

"Let me guess," said Dad. "Still not enough precision?"

"That's right. How did you know?" said a shocked Zack.

"It's simple really," Dad replied. "There isn't a game on earth that you boys can't master, so we knew the problem must be either the game or the hardware," he explained. "So we looked online, and not a single person has won a ticket using a console."

"So it's all a scam then?" said Fabio, looking furious.

"Not quite Fabio. A few tickets *have* been won, though only for the smallest passenger planes. But... they didn't use a console... They won using a Wicked Wings arcade machine! Not bad for the one-finger fumbler, eh," he concluded.

"Not bad at all," said Fabio. "So now we have to find somewhere that has one of those machines."

"Well grab your coats gang, 'cos I've just found one, and... they're hosting the competition too!" yelled Zack.

"It's that new arcade that's just opened up, called Quad-G, it's open 'til eleven o'clock so we still have time!"

"Quad-G, as in four G's?" asked Dad. "What do all those G's stand for?"

"**Games, Games, Games, and... Games**," replied Zack. "Four G's for four floors of ultimate gaming goodness. Just a single fee at the door, for all your gaming galore!"

"Oh dear," said Mum. "But it's my winding-down 'off-duty' time, not arcade adventure time," she continued. "But... these *are* exceptional circumstances, so... **Let's Go!**" and they grabbed their coats and scarves, and bolted to the car.

"**EARTHLINGS**... strap into your seats," said Zack.

"Start your engine," said Fabio.

"Beep... beep... beep..." said Dad

"**BEEEEEP!**" they all shouted, and they set off for the arcade.

"Daaaaad... any chance you remember the gamers that won the tickets?" Zack queried.

"There weren't many, but one did stick in my mind, called... JAY-17," he replied.

"**WHAT!!!**" shrieked Fabio and Zack, as they quickly

turned their heads to face each other... "**NOT THE JAYS!**"

"Don't worry about those cheaters," said Dad. "They've tried to beat you in two tournaments now, and failed both times!"

"You know what, you're right Dad," said Zack. "I'm not going to let those stinky cheating cheaters bother me any longer."

"Me neither," Fabio agreed. "Me neither."

When they arrived at the arcade, they tugged open the heavy double doors and were instantly hit with the sweet smell of candy floss and popcorn, then flashing screens and lights covering every inch of the walls, followed by an arcade orchestra, of retro rhythms, 8-bit beeps, 16-bit synths, and modern-gen music, all blasting out their mesmerizing memorable melodies.

As they gazed around in hypnotic awe, Fabio and Zack smiled the smiliest smiley smiles they had ever smiled before.

"Four tickets please," said Mum.

"Of course Madam, that'll be..."

"Not so fast young lady," a big man called out to the

cashier, as he waddled over with his shiny manager badge on his shirt, waving his finger. "Have you seen the time?"

"Oh dear," said Mum. "This is our first time here, are we too late?"

"Yes… you're way too late…" he paused.

Fabio and Zack inhaled for what was about to be a new world record Nooooo…

"You're way too late… tooooo… pay full price of course," the manager continued, with a huge smile. "And don't I recognise you boys from the local papers? Yes, yes, you're the one who won the BuilderDash tournament," he said, as he pointed at Fabio. "And you're the one who won the CataKarts tournament," and he pointed at Zack. "Give them the Late Arrivals discount to the power of four, multiplied by the square root of the New Comers discount, and add on two Local Legends discounts," he said to the teller.

"But Boss, however do I calculate all that?" fretted the young lady.

"Oh apologies," said the manager. "It's quite simple really, all you need to do is **jump** to that key, then **jump** to that one, then press the button with the **duck** on it, then **jump** to the one over there, then press that **dash** symbol, another press of the **duck** button, and finally **jump** to that key."

"So... jump, jump – duck, jump – dash, duck, jump?" she clarified, as she mimicked his movements.

"Perfect," said the manager, as Fabio smiled at the button combination.

"Oh dear, that comes to a negative number Boss," said the teller, after typing the discount combo.

"So it does," he said looking around. "Then that must mean they get free entry, and..." and he grabbed four bags of candy floss and handed them to Mum, Dad, and the boys. "There we go, that should cover it, so now all you need to do is Game, Game, Game and Game!"

"Thank you kind mister manager man," said Zack. "We're actually looking for one particular game, in particular. It's called Wicked Wings."

"I see," said the manager. "After winning some free flights are we?"

"Yes," replied Fabio. "We need them to help our friend; her grandma has just been rushed into hospital."

"Oh dear, that's terrible news; I hope she's going to

be okay," said the manager. "All competitions are on the top floor, so it's up there, but as you can imagine, it's the most popular game at the moment, so there's quite a wait to get on it. Just take a ticket from the clerk when you get there, and you can carry on gaming while you wait. They'll call you through the intercom when it's your turn. Good luck, and I hope you win your flights!"

"Thank you!" they all replied, then quickly raced upstairs.

"Wow!" said a stunned Dad, as he saw the huge professional looking machine jolting around on its hydraulics. "That looks amazing! With a name like Wicked Wings, I was expecting it to be more... erm... arcadey."

"It's literally the most hyped game out at the moment Dad," Zack explained. "So no expense was spared on this one."

"Good evening," said the Wicked Wings clerk. "My name's Bob. Apologies for the long wait times, but it looks like everyone in town is trying to win the free flights."

"Hi Bob," said Dad. "Is this simulator okay for

children, it's bouncing around like a fairground ride."

"Of course, they're the main target audience!" replied Bob. "Don't worry, they'll be all strapped in, and to keep the competition completely kid friendly, they won't even be transporting passengers, just a plane full of cargo!" he explained. "Now... will you all be having a go?"

"Erm... probably just the boys please," said Mum, looking at Dad, who nodded in agreement.

"Certainly, here you go then young men," and he passed them both a number for the queue.

"Five hundred and twenty five!" gasped Fabio, as he looked at the ticket. "What number is playing now?"

"Erm, that'll be ticket five hundred," Bob replied.

"And, how long does each game take?" Fabio queried further.

"Well, that all depends on how good they are... The actual flight time isn't very long, but getting in and out, explaining all the controls, and handing out tissues to all the upset faces when they lose, all adds up. We're probably squeezing in about 10 games per hour."

Fabio turned to his mum looking worried. "I don't think we'll have enough time to make it."

"Well..." said Bob, leaning in. "There *is* a way for you to win a lower number... if you're up for a challenge?" he queried, with a raised eyebrow.

"Challenge?" replied Zack. "Our lives are a non-stop emotional rollercoaster of challenges, so we're definitely up for that."

"Well you're going to love this then," said Bob. "We set up another competition on that machine over there; if you can beat someone, then you'll win their place in the queue."

The boys peered over to see it, but it was surrounded by a large crowd of gamers, so they dashed over for a closer look. As they got nearer they heard some familiar sounds, and when the machine came into view they both smiled...

06

BULLY

Fabio and Zack clapped their hands together, then rubbed them in excitement, as they cast their eyes on, none other than... the one and only... BuilderDash Arcade Machine!

Mum and Dad could see the boys needed some SERIOUS gaming time, and didn't want to embarrass or interrupt them, so they scurried off to explore the rest of the arcade, with Mum instantly drawn to a huge dance machine, and Dad managed to hunt down a dusty old A.X.E. machine, tucked away in a dimly lit corner.

"Challenger coming through," said Zack, pushing Fabio through the crowd. "Anyone that can beat my friend here, can have his ticket."

"What number?" asked one of the gamers.

"525," said Zack.

"Nah, not worth the risk, the place might've closed up before then."

"Okay, you can have my ticket too then," added Zack.

"What number?" asked another gamer?

"526," he replied.

"526! That's even worse!" he laughed, then all the other gamers began laughing at Zack too.

"I'll beat you blindfolded," said Fabio, nervously, but they didn't hear him with all the laughing. "**I'LL BEAT YOU BLINDFOLDED!**" he shouted, and the crowd suddenly went quiet.

"What level?" another gamer called out.

"Any," replied Fabio, drawing the attention of everyone around, as more gamers flocked over to see.

"Ha... Ya fink ya can beat *me* do ya?" laughed one of the bigger gamers, pushing his way through the crowd. "The name's Bully, an am the best BuilderDash player in 'ere, ain't no one can beat me," he boasted. "Ya see all them top scores," he said, prodding the screen on the arcade. "Yeah, they all say **BULLY**... Ya ain't got no chance kid."

"What's your ticket number?" asked Zack, not in the slightest bit fazed by Bully's efforts to scare them.

"501," replied Bully. "I'm up next, but that don't matter, 'cos I ain't gonna lose to a kid wiv a blindfold," he laughed again, looking around to get the other gamers laughing too.

Fabio pulled off his scarf and used it as a blindfold, as Zack guided him up to the machine.

"What level?" asked Fabio.

"Forty!" said Bully. "Bet ya couldn't beat this level even wivout a blindfold!" he mocked.

But Fabio just smiled and took the controls.

3... 2... 1... GO! And they were off.

Fabio executed a thunderous launch, taking an instant lead.

Jump, jump – duck, jump – dash, duck, jump... Fabio was on a flawless run and quickly increased the gap. He even took the risky road, nailed every jump, and landed the double dash at the end. He completely thrashed Bully, and the crowd began cheering as he took off his blindfold.

Bully looked around, and then stared down at Fabio, who was fully expecting him to make up some excuse why he lost, and not give him the ticket.

"Ya did good there kid," said Bully, putting his hand on his shoulder. "Ya did reet good in fact. I ain't never seen *anyone* go that fast before, ya some kinda pro or sumfink?"

"I'm the world champion," Fabio replied.

"Wow, that's awesome kid! I knew ya must be, 'cos only a world champ could beat *me!*" he laughed, though this time not to mock him.

"Here ya go kid, ya won this fair 'n' square," and he passed his ticket to Fabio.

"Thanks Bully!" said Fabio.

"No probs kid, and ya can call me Billy if ya likes, that's me real name, I just use Bully to scare the noobs!" he chuckled. "Anyway, how come ya needs to get on Wicked Wings so bad?"

Fabio pulled Billy and Zack away from the crowd, for a bit of privacy.

"A friend needs my help; her grandma has been rushed into hospital!" Fabio explained.

"Whoa, that's 'orrible news kid... My nanna means the world to me, so I tell ya what... I'm gonna help ya win all the tickets ya need... an I got the perfect plan to do it too..."

"A perfect plan you say," said Zack, as he glanced at Fabio and smiled.

"Aye, but there's just one catch... You'll have to gamble the ticket ya just won."

"But I can't do that," fretted Fabio. "I'm up next; they'll be calling me soon."

"But ya gonna needs more than one go kid," said Billy. "An if ya use the ticket now, then ya can't win any more."

"Billy's right," agreed Zack. "I know how good you are at gaming Fabio, and we'll probably beat this thing in less goes than anyone on the planet, but we *will* need more than one."

"Well listen up then, 'cos here's the plan," said Billy, lowering his voice. "Challenge another gamer on BuilderDash wiv ya 501 ticket, then when ya win, ya got two tickets! Then ya can have ya go on Wicked Wings and you'll still hava a ticket spare to win more wiv. Then just rinse and repeat."

"That's an awesome plan Billy!" said Zack. "You'll get loads of goes Fabio, 'cos every time you finish one, you can come back and win another on BuilderDash!"

"Aye, that's what I've been doing all day," said Billy. "But I still ain't won any flights... It's a tough game ya know... a reet tough game."

"I have to agree," said Fabio. "That *is* an awesome plan Billy."

"Thanks kid," Billy replied. "Now let's get back to BuilderDash, ya ain't got long 'til ya number's called."

They all sped back to the BuilderDash machine and attempted to execute Billy's plan. Fabio offered his 501 ticket, but after seeing him thrash Billy, no one wanted to play him, so the boys had to get creative...

They raised the stakes to all three tickets, offered them three chances, Fabio had to play with one hand behind his back, and finally, even if they lose, Fabio would still let them keep tickets 525 and 526!

Finally, a challenger walked over with ticket 502. "Ok mate, you've tempted me, but can I ask for just one more thing?"

"What is it?" asked Fabio.

"That you sign my BuilderDash cap," he replied, handing him a marker.

"Of course," said Fabio. "It would be my absolute pleasure," he beamed, as he scrawled his name on the cap.

"Right then, I'll look after the tickets while ya play," said Billy. "To make proper sure that no one backs out," and he reached out his open palm.

They dumped the tickets into Billy's hand, and rushed to start the three matches.

Fabio won the first and second game in no time, but just after they started the third, an announcement buzzed through the speakers...

"501 to Wicked Wings... 501 to Wicked Wings."

"Billy!" Fabio panicked, mid game. "Can you ask the clerk to wait a minute?" But there was no answer.

"Zack! Where's Billy?" Fabio fretted.

Zack looked around, but he was nowhere to be seen... Then he squinted over to the Wicked Wings machine, and saw Billy pass the tickets to the clerk, and then... get in.

"**Fabio!**" screamed Zack. "He's having a go on Wicked Wings! I can't believe it... HE TRICKED US!"

07

STINKY STEALING
STEALY STEALER

Fabio was in a complete frenzy and didn't know what to do. If he left the BuilderDash match, he would lose, but he was desperate to get to the Wicked Wings machine too. Just then, his opponent lifted his hand off the controls and raised them in the air.

"You win mate," he said. "Don't worry about finishing the level; it looks like Bully stole your tickets so you better get over there fast."

"Thanks man," said Fabio, and the boys double-dashed to Bob, waving their arms in distress.

"**Stop! Stop!**" they shouted. "Billy stole our tickets; it's supposed to be our turn now!"

"Billy stole your tickets? Now that can't be right," he challenged back. "I know he likes to tease the new players a bit..." but before he could continue, the door to Wicked Wings opened.

"Billy! How could you?" Fabio accused, sounding betrayed.

"What?!" Billy responded innocently.

"You stole our tickets so you could steal our turns, you... you... **stinky stealing stealy stealer!**" Fabio blurted out.

"Well that'll teach ya for trustin' strangers then won't it," Billy replied.

"See," said Fabio, turning to Bob. "He's just admitted it!"

"Well that *is* quite compelling evidence," Bob agreed. "However, I still can't possibly believe it."

"Why not?" cried Fabio and Zack in unison. "Why won't you believe us?"

"Well firstly, 'cos his dad owns the place, and secondly... *I* know what *really* happened..." Bob revealed.

"When Billy saw the last person leave the game, he rushed over, handed me your tickets, and pleaded me to wait for you. Then he asked if he could have a cheeky go while we waited. Now normally I'd have said no, but because he's so rubbish at the game, I thought *he'll only be in there for a few seconds,* so why not."

"*Heeey*, Uncle Bob," Billy complained jokingly. "I'm not *that* bad!" he giggled. "Okay... maybe I am."

"Oh Billy," said a red-faced Fabio. "We're so sorry, for accusing you of being a... stinky stealing stealy stealer and stealing our tickets."

"Please, don't worry about it," Billy replied. "But you have to admit, it was a pretty good lesson for not trusting strangers!"

"Yes it was," said Zack. "And we'll never do it again, but, hang on a second... your voice has changed."

"Yeah, that's just Bully's voice, the big scary gamer that likes to tease the new players, and teach them to not trust strangers! Anyway, enough explaining, you've got some flights to win!"

Fabio and Zack climbed into the cockpit, settled into the pilots' seats, and got ready at the controls.

"Wow, looks like you boys know what you're doing," said Bob. Have you played this game before?"

"Well, we've played *loads* of flight simulators," Fabio

replied. "So we know what all the controls and dials do."

"But the only problem is..." added Zack. "We've only ever played on consoles and computers, so this is our first time in a realistic cockpit," he explained.

"I see..." said Bob. "Well in that case, you may want to start off with one of the smaller planes... Which one do you need to win flights for?" he queried.

"Erm... the 854," replied the boys.

Bob paused for a moment looking a bit shocked... then a lot shocked... then *sooooo* shocked, that his eyebrows rose up almost above his head.

"Sorry, I must have misheard; I thought you said the 854 for a second there?" Bob chuckled, shaking away the shock.

"Yep, that's the one," smiled Zack.

"As in the... Double-Quad Engine, Triple-decker, Super MegaLiner... 854?" Bob clarified, still not believing his ears.

"The one and only," Fabio smiled too.

"But... but... that's the largest passenger plane in the world! The game was already on about a five-hundred percent difficulty, so that's just bumped it up to a cool thousand percent. You'll be needing some big-brain skills, and a huge airport, to have any chance of landing that monster in it," said Bob, as he selected the plane.

"Right, well that's that bit done. Now... which airport do you need?"

"*I'll* show you," Zack offered, as he yanked out his phone.

"Hmmm, that's odd," said Bob. "There must be something wrong with the images for that airport... All it's showing are pictures of this small road leading to a little building."

"That's no small road," said Fabio. "That's the runway!"

"Yes, and that's no little building either," added Zack. "That's the airport!"

Bob scrunched his eyes, then rubbed them, then squinted a few times as he looked at the images.

"But... but... we were already up to a thousand percent difficulty! Adding that tiny airport to the mix just bumped it up another nine thousand! So now you'll be needing... **Super Big-Brain 1o,000 Ultra IQ skills**, and a whole lotta luck!" Bob spluttered, almost falling back from a shock overload.

He selected the airport, shaking his head in disbelief,

then strapped them in and put on their aviation headsets "Right then young men, we're all set... Let me know when you're ready."

"**Ready!**" yelled Fabio.

"**Ready!**" squealed Zack.

"Then hold on tight boys, 'cos it's about to get real rocky," he warned, closing the door to the machine, and plunging Fabio and Zack into complete darkness.

08

WICKED WINGS

As Bob pushed the start button, the hydraulics juddered into action, then the sound of gale force winds, and loud rumbles of thunder, blasted through the cockpit speakers, and then the screens illuminated to reveal the horrendous storm, pounding away at the windscreen with snow, sleet, and hail.

Just a moment ago, the boys were in a fun-packed arcade, but the ultra realism of the cockpit, graphics, sound, and motion, had fully immersed them. Fabio and Zack were now the pilots of the ML854, and in terrifying danger.

The controls began to vibrate and shudder violently, making it difficult for Fabio to keep them steady, and their headsets crackled as they received an in-game transmission from ground control.

"Mike Lima 854, Tower Control Alpha here. **Attention! Attention!** Emergency protocol activated due to severe weather. **Warning! Warning!** Auto pilot deactivated as cannot safely navigate storm. **Sensor malfunction! GPS failure! Manual landing required!** I repeat, **Manual Landing Required!** Do you copy? Tower Control Alpha out."

The realism caused the boys to enter level-one panic, and beads of sweat began to form on their foreheads.

The game was awaiting voice confirmation, with a simple 'Message Received', but the immersion had plunged them into full flight mode, and all their previous flight-sim training took over.

"Tower Control Alpha, Mike Lima 854 here. Message received loud and clear," said Fabio. "Emergency protocol activated due to severe weather, auto pilot deactivated, sensor malfunction, GPS failure, manual landing required. Mike Lima 854 out."

Suddenly, their bodies jolted to the left, and then the right, as a gigantic gust of wind battered the plane, knocking it completely off course.

Fabio wrestled with the controls, trying desperately

to regain control, as Zack frantically flipped switches to help stabilise the plane.

Next, three blinding flashes of lightning forked through the angry thick grey clouds. The first bolted past them on the left, the second streaked to the right, but the third was aimed directly at the plane, and it hit them hard, with a loud sharp *CRACK!*

The shock caused the electrics to shut down, and the entire cockpit went black, leaving just a faint glow from a few emergency buttons.

The boys had now entered level-two panic... **Double-Sweat Danger**, and beads of sweat began forming on top of the beads of sweat!

Zack looked closely at the weather and noticed something very strange happening... The direction of the storm had changed... The snow, sleet, and hail, were no longer battering the windscreen, they were moving upwards at increasing speed, which could only mean one thing...

"**Free fall!**" Zack shouted in terror, as the plane plummeted, catapulting them into level-three panic... **Triple-Sweat Terror**, where the sweat on the sweat was now sweating.

Zack suddenly remembered a flight sim game, set in space, where an alien craft completely disabled his spaceship. The only way he survived was by getting the systems back online, and for that he had to reboot the ship's computer.

He wiped his drenched brows with his sleeve, took a deep breath, and quickly scanned the glowing emergency buttons, and there it was...

He flipped up the safety cover and slammed his palm down hard on the system-reboot button... At first nothing happened, then a second later, the lights in the cockpit flickered and the plane jolted back to life.

"**YES!!!**" they shouted, as Zack powered up four engines, and they quickly stabilised the plane.

"I can't see the landing strip!" Fabio wailed, and just then, another huge bolt of lightning streaked past them, followed immediately after by a deafening boom of thunder.

The flash briefly illuminated the cloud-filled sky, revealing something in the distance, through a slight break in the clouds... A faint line of lights...

"**The runway!**" Fabio exclaimed, as he fixed his gaze on the exact position and took a snapshot in his mind, before the clouds drifted back to block his view.

Fabio fought with the controls, against the feedback from the howling wind, as Zack shut down two engines, and gradually reduced the throttle, to slow and descend the plane.

As they dipped beneath the clouds, their visibility increased to a whopping... 0%, as although they were out of the clouds, an endless fog swept in.

"What are we going to do, we can't see the runway?" Zack howled.

"*I* can see it," Fabio replied, and he continued their approach towards his mental image of where it was.

"Are you ready for the wheels?" asked Zack.

Fabio clenched the flight stick tightly and nodded, so Zack grabbed the lever for the landing gear and pushed it down, but as the hatches opened and the wheels lowered, it altered the aerodynamics of the plane causing it to shudder uncontrollably and it knocked them slightly off track.

Fabio quickly realigned the plane, accounting for the impact from the landing gear, just as the faint lights of the runway gradually blinked into view through the fading haze.

They were just about to smile, when the fog suddenly swirled up high into the sky and quickly formed into a towering tornado, scooping up dust and debris from all around, then firing it out in all directions. And to make matters worse... the cyclone was spinning its way to the runway!

As they came into land, they battled with the controls with all their might, struggling to stabilise the plane as it collided with the violent twister, bombarding them with its cyclone of clutter.

They managed to make it to the runway, but the wheels crashed down hard onto the tarmac and buckled under the pressure. The front snapped off first, causing the nose of the plane to drop and graze along the ground, then the remaining wheels failed, and were severed off from the force.

Gradually, the plane slowed, as it scraped along the runway with sparks sparkling, and screeches screeching, from the grating, grinding metal, until finally... it came to silent stop.

Fabio and Zack slumped back into their seats, panting, sweating, and completely exhausted. They were still very much absorbed in all the realism, and for the briefest of moments, they truly believed they had just piloted and landed a real plane, against all the possible odds that one could ever possibly be against, and the hugest smile stretched across their faces.

Suddenly, the door to the machine opened, revealing the flashing lights and bustling sounds of the arcade, and it thrust them abruptly back to reality.

Their minds were not yet prepared for their amazing feat to be over, and the sudden shock left them feeling quite sad and taken back, when they realised it was all... just a game.

"Oh," said Fabio, sullenly. "For a moment there... I..."

"I know," said Zack, with a brave little smile, "Me too..."

They clambered out with their heads slightly dipped, as they struggled with their emotions, but as soon as their feet touched the ground... the room ignited with thunderous applause!

The boys glanced up and the entire floor had gathered around the game.

You see... It may have just been a game, but Fabio and Zack's amazing feat was the first time anyone in the arcade had seen a plane actually land, and the gamers were so excited that they huddled around the spectator screen to watch.

The boys received some well deserved pats on the back, as their smiles returned, and they thanked the crowd for their support, before returning to Bob for their results...

"Now then, Mister Bob," Fabio began. "I know it wasn't the prettiest of landings, but I do believe we just landed the hugest plane, in the teeniest airport, on the most insanest of difficulties, and... on our very first attempt!" he stated proudly.

"Sure, there may have been a few wheels missing," added Zack. "But technically, the plane *is* on the landing strip, well mostly anyway, so does that mean we've won the tickets?"

"Well young men, there's no denying that was a truly amazing feat," Bob praised. "And as you can see by the crowd, the spectators most certainly agree too, but... unfortunately I don't award the tickets myself. All attempts are automatically submitted online, and we just receive a pass, or a fail. Don't worry though, it doesn't take long," Bob smiled. "In fact, here are your results now... Your attempt has been marked as a..."

09

SILLY SMALLY SMALL PRINT

Fabio stood there with his hands cupped and hope in his eyes, along with a nail-biting Billy, a nervous Zack, and an audience of anticipation, with one gamer even grabbing a chair and sitting right on the edge of it.

"Your attempt has been marked as a... a..." Bob stuttered, looking around at all the little faces, before a frown formed on his own. "A fail, I'm afraid Fabio. It says you didn't meet the criteria, and that we need to read the small print at the bottom of the rules," he explained, grabbing the glossy rules sheet and pointing to the bottom.

"What small print?" Fabio challenged back. "The

only thing at the bottom of the rules is a thin faint underline."

Bob grabbed a magnifying glass and took a closer look.

"Yep... that's it," he replied. "That thin faint line *is* the small print! The first thing it says is 'To read this small print you will need the following: One Magnifying Glass' and it then goes on to say that to complete the challenge you must land with no damage to the plane. Now we can rerun the footage again, but I'm pretty sure there may have been a slight bit of damage to the wheels and the odd little scrape," he concluded, in the understatement of the century!

Fabio and Zack felt their whine-o-meters rapidly increasing, to levels not even all the wine in France could contend with, but somehow they managed to contain it, and regain their composure.

"Well if that's the way they want to play it," said Fabio. "Then... Challenge Accepted!" and he nodded sharply, with a determined look on his face.

"Bob... we'll be needing another go," said Zack. "And I do believe you already have our ticket 502."

"I certainly do young men," replied Bob, with a smile,

and he helped them back into the machine.

"But Fabio!" cried Billy. "That's your last one; you won't have any tickets left to win more goes with!"

"Don't worry Billy; my brain has cracked this game now so we won't need another go," Fabio reassured him, as the door closed.

In their second attempt, their piloting roles perfectly complemented each other, and they countered every gust of wind, dodged every bolt of lightning, and flew so fast, that they got to the runway before the tornado even had chance to form, in what appeared to be a flawless run.

"There we go," boasted the boys, as they scrambled out of the machine. "Not a scratch on her." And the growing crowd cheered again.

"That was amazing!" said Bob, giving them a huge thumbs up. "That must be a pass, for sure."

"Well there's no damage," said Zack. "So unless they invented some new rules in the past few minutes, then we've got this one in the bag."

"I completely agree," said Bob. "And here are the results now... Your second attempt has been marked as a... **WHAT???!!!**"

"**What is it?**" shouted the entire floor.

"**A fail!!!**" howled a completely shocked Bob. "It says you didn't meet the criteria again, and this time we need to read the smaller-than-small print, located below the small print," Bob explained.

Billy grabbed the rule sheet. "But Uncle Bob, there's nothing under the small print... just a blank space."

"Then based on their first small-print trick, I'm guessing the smaller-than-small print is hiding right in that blank space," he replied. "Just give me a minute..."

Bob brought up the online version of the rules on his laptop, increased the zoom to maximum and noticed a faint smudge, he then whipped out his phone, snapped an image and did a maximum zoom on that, and there it was... The smaller-than-small print!

"I've found it," said Bob. "The first thing it says is: 'To read this smaller-than-small print you will need the following: One Microscope' and it then goes on to say that to complete the challenge you must also land with 100% cargo remaining."

"Those sneaky cheaters," complained Zack. "Offering a prize, but then making it impossible to win with their sneaky cheating small print."

"Yeah," Fabio agreed. "I thought I saw something falling from the back of the plane… it must have been the cargo."

"Right then Uncle Bob, we'll be needing another go," said Billy.

"Certainly Billy, here you go," and he passed him another ticket… Ticket number 539!!!

"But Uncle!" Billy whined. "That's way too high, we need another go now!"

"But I have all these other gamers, waiting for their turn. I can't give you special treatment just because we're related, and your dad owns the place," explained Bob. "That wouldn't be fair on all the others."

"I understand Uncle," replied a defeated Billy, as he dipped his head and began to wander off, slowly dragging his feet. "Come on guys," he gestured to Fabio and Zack. "I don't know how, but we're gonna have to win some more tickets."

Just before they walked off, they heard a little voice call out from the group of spectators. "Mr Fabio!"

They looked back, but couldn't see who it was.

"Mr Fabio… wait!"

And just then, a little boy nudged his way to the front of the crowd.

"I'm' really sorry Mr Fabio, but I overheard you talking earlier, and you need the flights to help someone's Nana."

"That's right young man," replied Fabio, kneeling down to meet the boy's height. "Our friend's Grandma was rushed into hospital and we need to get there and help."

"Well I love my Nana lots and lots so I want you to have my ticket," and the little boy passed his ticket to Fabio... It was number 503!

"Are you sure young man?" asked Fabio. "It's your go next."

"Yes, I'm very, very sure," said the boy. "My go won't save anyone's Nana, but if I give it to you then it could."

Then another child came forward and offered theirs... then another... and another... until they had all the goes they could possibly need.

Fabio and Zack felt quite overwhelmed with emotion, from the selfless kindness of these complete strangers. "Thank you all so much," they said, with their tear-filled eyes, and they climbed back into the machine.

They had go, after go, after go... getting perfect landings every time, but no matter what they tried, they could not land the plane with 100% cargo remaining.

The insane difficulty of the competition had the cargo door set to: **BROKEN**, and it was jammed open just enough for boxes to fall out from the gap at the bottom.

After countless failed attempts, it was now closing time and Bob submitted their final run... But just as all the others did, it came back as Failed.

"That **Stupid... Cheating... Game!**" shouted Billy, as he stomped off, angry and upset.

Fabio and Zack trudged off too, with their heavy stomping feet, as they went to find their parents.

In complete contrast to the boys, Mum and Dad had been having an absolute blast in the arcade. Mum had been on the dance game all night, made a few dance-gamer friends, and even got her name on the scoreboard, as TDM... The Dancing Mum. And Dad had attracted a little crowd himself, as he completely obliterated the top score on the A.X.E. machine!

As Fabio and Zack arrived, Mum could see from their faces that they had not been successful, but she wanted to remain positive.

"How did you get on boys?" she asked. "Did you manage to land the plane?"

"Yes," replied Fabio. "But the **Silly Smally Small Print** said we failed because there was damage to the plane."

"Yeah," added Zack. "And then we had another go and did a perfect landing but then the **Sillier-than-Silly,** and **Smallier-than-Small Print** failed us because we lost some cargo."

"But everyone was so kind when they found out our cause, and gave us all their tickets, so we could have every turn until closing time," Fabio explained. "But nothing we tried worked."

"Oh my dearest boys, I'm so sorry," Mum said lovingly. "It's really late now though, and you both look terribly tired. I don't think there's anything else we can do tonight, so let's get a good night's sleep and we can try again tomorrow morning," she smiled, and gave them both a big hug.

They made their way to the exit and were just about to leave when...

"**Fabio... Zack... Wait!!!**" shouted a voice...

10

UPSIDE DOWN

They looked around and saw Billy tearing towards them, flailing his arms to get their attention. Mum and Dad looked a little confused, but Fabio and Zack were happy to see him, as they hadn't had a chance to say goodbye after he stomped off.

"Hi Billy," said the boys, as they waved back.

"Mum, Dad, this is Billy, we made friends upstairs, his dad owns the place," they explained.

"Hello Billy," said Mum. "It's such a pleasure to meet a friend of the boys. You're a very lucky young man you know, to have such a wonderful arcade," she complimented."

"Yes," echoed Dad. "I couldn't agree more, this place is awesome, it's quite possibly every kid's dream," he added.

"Thanks Miss," Billy smiled at Mum. "And thanks Sir," he nodded at Dad. "Yes, it's super cool having this place, and I love all the machines we have... apart from that cheating Wicked Wings and its silly smally small print stopping Fabio and Zack from winning the flights," he grumbled. "But... I have some urgent information for you... I stomped off to explain the situation to my dad, and without a second thought, he said we can..." and Billy leaned in close so no one could overhear. "Keep the arcade open all night so you can carry on trying," he whispered excitedly.

"Oh my goodness," gasped Mum. "That's ever so kind," she added. "We couldn't possibly refuse such a generous offer, could we boys."

"Nope," they replied, as their tired eyes suddenly widened with excitement.

"Awesome!" replied Billy. "Wait at reception, until everyone else leaves, and I'll tell my dad. He can't wait for someone to beat that game. He thinks he'll get a free column in the local paper, if someone finally wins. And he wants to help too of course!"

Billy's dad, and his uncle Bob, arrived at reception

just after closing time, waved off the last customers, locked up, and lowered the blinds.

"Right then," said Billy's dad. "It's lovely to see you all again, I hope you've enjoyed your night at the arcade," he smiled. "You've already met my son Billy, I'm Barry, and this is my brother Bobby, or Uncle Bob, as Billy calls him."

"Either's fine," smiled Bob.

"Now, I hear time is against us, sooooo... let's get this party started!" howled Barry. "I'll grab us all some drinks and snacks, to keep us going, and Bobby will take you back to the wickedly wicked Wicked Wings. I'm desperate to see someone finally beat that thing; it'll do wonders for our publicity, and from what Billy's told me, Fabio and Zack are the duo to do it!" he beamed. "Though please know, it's not *all* business... there's a heart in here somewhere," he said, patting his chest. "So I'd have been happy to help regardless," and he trotted off to gather their gaming fuel.

The boys played deep into the night, having game after game, discussing strategies in between, and they executed every plan they could think of, but no matter what they tried... they couldn't stop the cargo falling out.

By 2am the boys were getting very, very tired, and when they fell asleep at the controls, Mum and Dad decided it was time to call it a night.

They thanked, Barry, Bobby, and whispered a thank you to a sleeping Billy, then started on their drive home.

With Dad at the wheel, Mum was watching Fabio and Zack in the rear-view mirror, and saw two very tired, arms crossed, frowny-faced boys, so she turned to face them.

"My dearest boys," she began. "I can see you're unhappy and I completely understand, but it's not even been a day since you got the news about Elle's yiayia, and you've already tried *so* much, and *so* hard to help."

"We know," they replied, fighting their heavy eyelids to glance up at Mum. "But it's not enough."

"We've found a way to use our gaming skills to help people in need," added Zack. "So now we want to help all the people, in all the needs."

"And that's a truly amazing attitude boys, but sometimes no matter what you do, not everyone can be helped, but you still have to let yourselves be happy, and take joy in all the times you *do* help people, like you did for us," explained Mum, putting a hand on Dad's shoulder. "So think about how much you helped us for a moment, and let's see if we can turn those frowns upside down.

Suddenly, Fabio and Zack jolted up straight in their seats. "Upside... Down," they mumbled in unison.

Then they turned to face each other and their eyes widened... "**UPSIDE DOWN!!!**" they yelled in delight!

"What is it boys?" asked a startled Mum.

"Mum, you're a genius, that's what!" Fabio blurted out in excitement.

"Dad, turn around quick!" Zack ordered. "We need to get back to the arcade, we'll explain on the way."

Dad knew the boys, and knew they had a new plan, so he headed back without question.

"Fabio, Zack, what is it? What's so important about upside down?" quizzed Mum, desperate for the answer.

"You've solved the game!" they replied. "You've solved the Wicked Wings competition!"

"We couldn't win because the cargo always escaped through the broken cargo door," Fabio explained.

"Yes," added Zack. "And the gap is at the **BOTTOM** of the door."

"Exactly," Fabio continued. "But if the gap was **UPSIDE DOWN**, then the cargo wouldn't fall out."

"I see," said Mum. "So you have to turn the cargo door upside down?" she asked, still confused.

"No," they replied. "That's impossible... But we can turn the... **PLANE UPSIDE DOWN!**" they celebrated. "Then we simply roll it back around just before landing."

"**BOYS!**" shouted Mum and Dad. "That sounds amazing! Do you think you'll be able to pull off a stunt like that?" they asked, as they pulled up to the arcade.

"With the amount of goes we've had, I think we can do anything on that game," they replied with confidence.

They all jumped out of the car in haste and ran to the entrance, but the metal security shutters were down, and the lights were off.

Fabio and Zack knocked a few times, with the sound of rattling iron echoing around the empty buildings, but there was no answer.

They dashed to the back, but the lights were off there

too, and the boys became panicked and distressed.

"It's okay," said Mum, comforting them. "We'll come back first thing tomorrow morning, I promise. What time do they open?"

Zack checked his phone, but became increasingly upset. "It's closed," he said, as a tear rolled down his cheek. "I can't believe it," he wept. "We finally solved the game, but we were too late, and now we can't help."

Mum knew there was nothing more she could say to cheer them up, they just needed a bit of time to work through their feelings, so instead, she sat in the back with them for the ride home, with one under each arm, and they cuddled up silently.

As they approached the turning for their street, Dad drove straight past it, and winked at Mum in the rear-view mirror.

"I think you've missed our turning Dad," mumbled a sleepy Zack.

"I know, but I've just had a Super Silly, Mega Massive Monster idea," he began. "You see... it's already silly-o-clock, the perfect time for Super Silly ideas, and we're already up and out, so I thought *surely a few more minutes wouldn't hurt,*" he explained. "So... we're popping to the... **Mega Massive Monster store** to reward you both for all your hard work. They may have a game there that'll put a smile on your faces."

As late as it was, and as tired and unhappy as they were, this is still Fabio and Zack we are talking about, and Fabio plus Zack plus Games equals... Very, VERY, **VERY**, Interested!

"Ok Dad," said Zack, "You've got our attention... but won't the store be closed at this super silly-o-clock hour?"

"Maybe a normal store," Dad replied. "But this is the Mega Massive Monster store! It's open twenty-four hours!"

"Interesting," said Fabio, rubbing his chin.

"Yes, very interesting indeed," said Zack, doing the same.

"We do have a few games on our wish lists," added Fabio.

"And... we *have* been working really, *really* hard," added Zack.

"Well I'm glad you agree as we're here now," said Dad, as he parked outside the entrance and turned off the engine, in the eerie looking, and almost empty, Mega Massive Monster car park.

"Does anyone actually do their shopping at this time of night?" asked Fabio, as a sharp breeze rustled a few branches in a lonely tree.

"A few do," replied Mum, raising her arms. "And they call them..." she continued, sticking out her fingers. "**The NightShoppers!**" she said, in a spooky whispering shout, and suddenly tickled the boys until they giggled.

"And when you stay at Fabio's" added Dad, in *his* spooky voice, staring at them in the rear-view mirror. "Sometimes *I* become a... **NIGHTSHOPPER!**" he howled, and quickly turned to face them with a scary face and twisted fingers.

"**Aaaaaarrrrrggggghhhhh,**" squealed the boys, in a laughing fright.

"Okay," said Dad, "*I'll* need to go in first, to see how scary the NightShoppers are. If everything's okay, I'll come and get you, but if I'm not back in **FIVE** minutes... it may mean... The NightShoppers have got me!" and he jumped out and dashed into the store.

Mum clicked the doors locked and they waited in silence, with Fabio and Zack staring at their watches, getting more and more concerned, the closer and closer it got to five minutes.

Four minutes and fifty-nine seconds later, Dad returned to the car and knocked on the window, signalling for Mum to open the door.

"We can go in boys, but the NightShoppers are quite scary tonight so you'll have to wear blindfolds until we get to the Game Zone," explained Dad.

They blindfolded the boys with their scarves, held their hands, and guided them straight to the gaming section.

"Are you ready for us to take off the blindfolds?" asked Dad.

"Erm, we're actually a bit scared now," they replied, squeezing Mum and Dad's hands.

"But we do need games," added Fabio.

"Yes," agreed Zack. "Hmmm... to scare or to game, now that is the question," he added.

"Gaming wins!" they yelled. "Sooooo... we're ready!" and Mum and Dad whipped off the scarves.

The boys inhaled sharply, ready for a super-powered super screaming session, and saw a huge white ghost towering in front of them, flailing violently.

"**Aaaaarrrrrgggghhhhh**, a **NightShopper!**" they shrieked, but then suddenly stopped...

11

CHOCCOBERRYNAANANILLA

As the shock quickly wore off, the boys realised they had just fallen victim to the dreaded... Super-Scare-Sight! When you see something you **think** is super scary, but only because you were *expecting* to see it.

You see... the towering white NightShopper ghost was actually just a huge white dust sheet, covering something equally huge. And the angry flapping was just a blast of air hitting the sheet, from the air ducts above.

Fabio and Zack looked around at the sparse scattering of customers.

"*Daaaaad,*" Zack complained. "I don't see *any* scary NightShoppers."

"Yeah Mum," Fabio whined. "All I see are

NiceShoppers! But congratulations to you both, on a top-notch, Fabio-approved, **JUMP SCARE!**"

"Thanks Fabio!" they replied.

"Now about that game I mentioned," said Dad, waving over to the Game Zone clerk.

"Hello young men, I remember you," he said, as he shuffled over. "I do get a bit muddled now and then, but I never forget a face," he added. "You are... Fart Master Fabs," he said, pointing at Zack. "So you must be... Lord Findington of Scrollville," and he pointed at Fabio.

"Hello," they replied.

"You're really close," added Zack. "But it's just the other way around, and... I've levelled up to Earl now too!"

"Ah yes, of course, I remember now," said the clerk. "And congratulations on levelling up!"

"Kind mister store guy?" Fabio probed.

"Yes young man," he replied.

"Last time we saw you, you were working in the day, and now you're working in the night. When do you ever get chance to sleep?" he asked.

"Well Mr Fart Master, the thing is, I'm not supposed to be working nights at all, but the game guy, Guy, called in sick, so I offered to cover his shift."

"The game guy guy?" queried Zack. "Don't you just mean the game guy?"

"No, the game guy, **Guy**... The game guy is called **Guy**." The clerk chuckled.

"Ahhhhh, I get it now," giggled Zack.

"So boys... I hear you've been working really hard to help someone," asked the clerk.

"That's right Sir," they replied.

"Well my favourite customer here... **ACE**," the clerk began, patting Dad on the shoulder. "Rushed in and asked if I could prepare a quick gaming surprise for you both, so..." and he grabbed a corner of the huge dust sheet, and began counting down. "Three... two... one... **SURPRISE!!!**" he yelled, and pulled away the sheet.

The sight was completely unexpected for the boys, and a wave of emotion hit them, knocking them back a little, and their eyes became glazed with tears.

They ran over and hugged Dad, then the clerk, and then Mum, littering them with a thousand thank yous, and extra thank-you sprinkles.

"**How?**" they cried.

"Well," Dad began, taking a deep breath. "Seeing you

both so upset, I needed to find a solution **FAST!** And my first thought was the Monster Store, but to prevent any further upset I didn't mention anything, in case they didn't have it, so as soon as Mum came up with the utterly brilliant scary NightShoppers, I used it to get in without raising any suspicion. I quickly explained our challenge to the clerk, and being the awesome guy he is, he was more than happy to help, so here we are... standing before us... another... Wicked Wings machine!!!" he spluttered, just managing to finish *his* WordSplosion!

"Mum... Dad... We're going to need a sweet treat to keep us awake for this one," said the boys, rubbing their hands together, excited to get back into the pilots' seats.

"Of course," said Dad. "Milkshakes all round. Now, do you want Chocolate, Strawberry, Banana, or Vanilla?" he asked.

"Hmmm," they pondered. "There's only one milkshake that will do for this challenge... The ultimate milkshake combo... The... **Chocco-berry-naana-nilla!**" they yelled.

"Ooh, that sounds tasty," said the grown-ups.

"Then Choccoberrynaananillas, all round," agreed

Dad, and he darted off to get them.

Fabio and Zack climbed into the machine and had a few practise runs, to get used to flying the plane upside down, and by the time Dad arrived back with the shakes, they were ready for a proper run.

The boys downed their shakes, licked their lips and signalled to the clerk with a big thumbs-up... They were ready.

The door closed, plunging them back into darkness, and the machine shuddered fiercely to life, with the harrowing sounds of the storm sending chills down their spines.

After their communication with tower control, they immediately rolled the plane upside down, securing the cargo firmly in place, and fought against the storm with all the strength in their hearts.

Flying upside down meant that left was now right, right was now left, up was now down, and down was now up, but that didn't faze them in the slightest, and once again, they battled against every blast of wind, swerved every streak of lightning, and countered everything the game could throw at them, until the landing strip was finally in sight.

Just moments before touchdown, Zack slowed and lowered the landing gear, Fabio rolled the plane back, and they executed a flawless finish.

The door opened to applause from Mum, Dad, and the clerk, along with a few nice NightShoppers, that had stopped by to see what all the excitement was about.

Fabio and Zack vaulted out of the machine, and began jumping around with joy, as this was their run-of-all runs-of-all runs! And they knew no amount of silly smally small print could fail them this time.

As they awaited their results, the tension was mounting. And despite their confidence, the boys couldn't help feeling anxious.

"Ah-ha, here we go," said the clerk, as the results pinged through. "Your attempt has been marked as a... a... A PASS!" he hollered.

"**WooHoo!**" cheered the boys, jumping around again, stopping in between for some of their signature victory poses, as Mum and Dad took some snaps.

"I can't believe it," the boys cried. "We're going to the tourney!"

I can't believe it," echoed Mum and Dad. "We're going

to Cyprus!"

"Congratulations boys," said the clerk. "I just need an email address now, to send the flights and everything else to."

After Mum filled in the details, they thanked the clerk a few more times, then rushed home for a well earned nap, and the moment their sleepy heads hit their soft fluffy pillows, they fell fast asleep. But... just a few measly hours later, it was already time to wake up and start packing, as take-off was scheduled for four o'clock and they had a whole week to pack for!

While the grown-ups frantically packed, Fabio got a clipboard, pad, and pencil, and made Fabio's Journey Checklist, containing: Taxi, Terminal, Check-in, Security, Boarding, and Take off. He then joined Zack for some gaming before it was time to leave.

Mum kept checking her emails for the flights, but there was nothing in her in-box, and they didn't have time to sit and wait. Once they were all packed and ready to go, they left for the airport.

On the way, Mum continued checking her emails, but still nothing, Fabio put his first tick in the Taxi check-box, then he and Zack texted the girls to let them know they were on their way and should be arriving in the evening.

"OMG Zack!!! Can't wait to see you! x." Elle messaged back.

"We won't get there til Monday morning as our flight takes forever, so I'll see you at the tourney. I'm so excited to meet you Fabio! x." Katsumi texted.

They arrived at the terminal, expecting the usual hustle and bustle of noisy crowds, rattling luggage, and barely audible airport announcements, but instead, they were met with something very strangely strange and very oddly odd... The exact opposite!

Apart from a sparse scattering of staff, the place was completely empty...

12

SPAM!

They stood staring blankly, at what should have been a very busy terminal, and they quickly became worried that somehow, they may be in the wrong place.

"Excuse me, how can I assist you today?" came a strange voice from nowhere.

They looked around in confusion, as the only thing surrounding them was a sea of digital check-in terminals.

"Excuse me, how can I assist you today?" the voice repeated.

"Who are you?" asked Zack.

"I'm SAD," the voice began, but before it could continue, Zack interrupted.

"Well come out from where you're hiding then and

we'll help cheer you up," he said, searching around for them.

"Apologies, but you misunderstood," the ghostly voice responded. "I'm a SAD BoT, a Super Awesome Digital Boarding Terminal. Please, ask me any question so I can assist you."

They all looked down and realised it was coming from one of the check-in terminals.

"Okay then," said Zack. "Where is everyone?"

"If you're referring to all the staff," the machine responded. "They have almost all been replaced with us SAD BoTs. We have been programmed to do everything a human can."

"Oh Really," Mum joined in, with a challenging tone. She doesn't mind most technology, but robots replacing humans really gets on her nerves. "Ok then, can you smile?"

"I'm sorry, I don't understand, please ask a different question," the terminal responded.

"Yeah, didn't think so," said Mum.

"Yeah, and you didn't answer my question either," Zack added. "I wasn't talking about the staff, I was asking where all the passengers were."

"I'm sorry, I don't understand, please ask a different question," the terminal responded.

"We don't have time for this nonsense," barked Zack, and he dashed through the sea of terminals, as the eerie echo of all their disturbing voices asked to help. But he ignored them all, and instead ran to the last remaining actual *human* check-in assistant, a super smartly-dressed lady, with the biggest, most beautiful smile he had ever seen.

"Excuse me Miss, but is this the right terminal for the Double-Quad Engine, Triple-decker, Super MegaLiner 854," he asked.

"It certainly is Sir," she replied.

"Then Miss... Where is everyone?" he queried, with his palms up, and a puzzling shrug so large, his shoulders were almost above his head!

"Well," the assistant began. "You may not know this, but there's a huge gaming tournament in Cyprus, starting tomorrow, and the entire plane was booked by the organisers for the tournament hosts, staff, and cargo. So the reason it's so empty here, is that they're all packed into the Super Elite Priority lounge, and board from their own Super Elite Priority gate.

"Thanks Miss," said Zack, and he waved the others over to the desk, and explained the mystery of the empty terminal.

As the smiling assistant began checking them in, Fabio marked the second tick on his checklist.

"There we go," she said, handing boarding passes to Zack and his dad. "All checked in! You just need to make your way through security now, as passengers are already boarding." She then turned and smiled at Mum. "I just need *your* details now please Madam."

Mum nervously checked her emails again, but still nothing, so she explained the situation to the assistant.

In a desperate effort to help, Fabio, Zack, and Dad got out their phones and called the competition organisers, the Wicked Wings head office, and the Monster store, but after battling through the annoying automated services, they were just plonked on indefinite hold.

"I'm really sorry Madam, I wish there was something I could do, but without the electronic tickets, you won't be able to fly," the lady apologised, losing her smile.

Mum looked at Zack and Dad. "You're going to have to continue on without us."

"But... but... I can't... I can't do this without Fabio,"

cried Zack, in a panic.

"Zack, Elle needs you, you have to go," said Fabio. "I'll stay on hold, and as soon as I get through, we'll get all this sorted and we'll be right behind you."

"They're right," said Dad. "We can't help Elle from here," and he grabbed Zack's hand and guided him off to security, though Zack just kept looking back at Fabio and his mum, with his hand reached out, until they were through, and out of sight.

As the final boarding announcement barked through the speakers, Mum hung her head in defeat. She knew there was no way they could get there in time.

"**MADAM QUICK!!!**" the assistant suddenly shouted, startling Fabio and Mum... "**SPAM!!!**" she yelled again.

"Thanks Miss, but I checked the spam folder, look," Mum replied, showing her phone to the lady.

"Wow that's a whole lotta spam," the assistant gasped. "But look at the time on them, it's all brand new spam! Quick, check the older pages."

Mum flicked back a few pages and there they were... the electronic tickets! They were there all along, but when Mum entered her details at the Monster store...

she forgot to deselect that sneaky little box, that allows companies to send you extra emails, so her spam folder had been bombarded with all sorts of stuff, pushing the flights email back a few pages.

The assistant rubbed her hands together and cracked her fingers, as she prepared for a record breaking check in.

"Right, let's do this," she said, and she began typing so fast, her fingers were just a blur. "Aaaaand Done!" she concluded, a few seconds later, smiling at her new personal best. "Now get to security **QUICK**... erm, I mean, QUICK please!"

"But what about our boarding passes?" Mum panicked.

"They're still printing, but you don't have time to wait, I'll fly them over as soon as they're done."

"Thanks Miss," Fabio and Mum shouted back, as they dashed to the security gate.

The smiling assistant waved over to the security team and gave them a few coded hand gestures, which when decoded mean: Super Speed Security Sweep required, Boarding Gate Closing. Then she quickly folded the boarding passes into paper aeroplanes and threw them over.

The security team nodded and then prepared for *their* personal best, as Fabio and Mum Darted through the Detector, got Whizzed over with the Wand, crammed the Carry-on through the Conveyor, and finished just in time to jump up and catch the boarding passes.

They ran as fast as they could, to the closing boarding gate, but by the time they reached it, it had already closed.

"Miss please... let us through," Fabio wailed, to the lady at the gate.

"I'm terribly sorry Sir, I wish I could, but the jet bridge has already detached from the plane," she apologised, pointing out of the window. "Can you see it?"

Fabio peered out of the window and saw the long tunnel, that connects the gate to the plane, retracting, and as the wheels of the plane began to move, his eyes began to fill with tears.

He lifted his clipboard and put a little tick in the Check-in box, and another in the Security box, but then he slowly scrawled a deep huge cross through the

Boarding box, carving it into the paper, and causing the pencil lead to snap from the force. He then dropped his arms, and the checklist and pencil fell from his hands and crashed to the ground, as the sound echoed around the room.

Mum's heart ached with sorrow for her little treasure, seeing him so upset, and her stomach filled with the deepest regret as she felt completely to blame.

"I'm so sorry my dearest Fabio; this is all my fault," she wept. "You fought so hard to get us here, and I ruined it at the last hurdle, with such a stupid mistake."

Fabio realised what Mum was trying to do, so he closed his eyes, pursed his lips, and took a deep breath in through his nose, in an attempt to reboot, and force away his upset.

"Sorry Mum," he replied, reboot successful. "But I don't accept your apology."

"I understand my dear," she said, dipping her head in shame. "I don't feel like I deserve forgiveness right now either."

"No Mum... you *don't* understand," he countered, glancing up and into her eyes. "You see... I know I love games... but this is one game I simply refuse to play."

"What game?" Mum queried.

"The blame game of course!" Fabio replied. "I will not, nope, never, not-a-chance, no thanks, N to-the-O to-the-T... NOT, allow you to blame yourself... and we're not blaming anyone else either, as the blame game is a pointless game that could go on forever, and the worst part is... nobody even wins!" he added. "We could blame all the companies that sent you spam, or blame your email company for putting the flights email into the spam folder in the first place. We could blame the competition for the small print, that failed my first attempt, or the smaller-than-small print that failed my second. We could blame Zack's email company for putting *his* emails into *his* spam folder, or blame Zack for not knowing to look there. Or... we could even blame the hospital for not having one of those special machines! You see Mum... there's no end to the blame game, and nobody ever wins! So... If we're going to focus on anything, then it's not going to be the one thing you didn't do, it's going to be all the things you did do!" and he ran into her arms and hugged her. "Thank you Mum, thank you for all the awesome things you do," and they stood there, watching helplessly from the window as the plane slowly crawled away.

But then something completely unexpected happened...

"Muuum?"

"Yes, my dearest Fabio."

"Shouldn't the plane be speeding up?" he asked.

"Yes, it should," replied Mum.

"Then why is it... slowing down?"

And they watched with confusion as the plane slowed to a halt...

13

AIRPORTOPIANS!!!

At first nothing happened, but then a door on the plane opened, revealing a figure wearing a black and metallic-grey robotic bodysuit, pulsing red with anger. The figure pointed at an airstair, and ordered it to drive to the door at once, and the moment it connected with the plane, the metallic figure stormed down the steps, followed by a huge crowd, and they all marched towards the boarding lounge.

"Hang on a minute," said Mum. "I remember that feisty female... She's the host from the CataKarts tournament."

"That's right Mum, it's Sixteen!" said Fabio, getting excited.

"Oh no, it's Sixteen!" fretted the airport staff, getting

scared. "And that menacing red pulse on her armour means she's angry!" and they all scrambled for a hiding spot.

The doors to the lounge burst open and Sixteen thundered in, followed by a stampede of staff.

"**AIRPORTOPIANS!!!**" she commanded. "Could someone please explain why there are two very special earthlings missing from my flight."

The airport staff were too scared to answer, but a sneaky one pushed another in front of Sixteen, forcing her to reply.

"Erm, we're very... sorry... Madam," stuttered the assistant, as she shuffled back. "Please accept our most sorriest apologetic apologies, but we had to close the gates when the jet bridge detached."

"I understand," Sixteen calmly replied, as she spotted all the terrified staff, and the pounding red light on her chrome armour softened to a gentle glowing blue. "I *can* be a little reasonable you know, on the rarest of oddest occasions, and I can see that you were all just doing your jobs, so please come out from your hiding places... I promise I won't bite."

The airport staff glanced around nervously for a

moment, then cautiously emerged.

"**BUT!**" Sixteen continued, causing them to wince back again. "I just need you to understand that this amazing young man here is one of my most treasured champions," she said, placing an arm around Fabio. "And not just because he's an amazing gamer... but because of the amazing reasons he's been entering tournaments. You see... he doesn't do it for fame and fortune... he does it to help people... people in need, and his team need him in this tournament so they can win funds for a life-saving hospital machine.

"That's right Miss, that *is* why we're going," said Fabio, hugging Sixteen's metallic arm. "But... how did you know?"

"Well, you see... my *other* most treasured champion told me... didn't you," she replied, and her crowd of staff parted, revealing Zack, with his dad standing proudly behind. "As soon as Zack spotted me on the plane, he rushed over and quickly explained what was going on, so I immediately ordered the plane to stop."

"Oh my, we're terribly sorry Madam," the assistant apologised again. "We should have confirmed with you that *all* your passengers were safely on board before takeoff. We're realigning the jet bridge with the plane as we speak, so you can all reboard very soon, and as a gesture of goodwill," she paused, getting out a super-special key, and unlocking a super-secret cupboard. "Please accept four of our Golden Galactic Gaming Globetrotter cards," and she handed one each to Fabio, Zack, Mum and Dad. "These super-special secret cards will grant you travel to all the gaming competitions you'll ever need to enter... and completely free of charge of course!"

"Wow! Thank you super-special super-kind Miss," said Fabio. "These cards will allow us to help even *more* people than we ever dreamed we could."

"That's right!" added Zack. "Your gift to us, is a gift to all the people we help, so thank you so much, Miss."

"Well it's the least we can do, to assist you in your generous gaming adventure," the Airport lady smiled, and she picked up Fabio's clipboard and broken pencil. "Oh dear, we seem to have a couple of little problems here... There's an error on the boarding check-box," so she rubbed out the cross, leaving just the visible impression. "And... your pencil appears to be broken," so she reached into her blazer pocket and pulled out a shiny new airport pen. "There we go young Sir," and she passed them to Fabio. "Ah-ha, perfect timing... the jet bridge has connected now, so you can all reboard. Good luck in the tournament!"

"Thanks again Miss," they replied, and they made their way to the plane.

They were greeted by an air hostess, also sporting a beamingly beautiful smile, who directed them to where they would be sitting, in what appeared to be the most luxurious cabin they had ever seen. It had much more First than First Class, so they named it... Firster Class!

"Excuse me Miss," Mum politely asked. "As much as I'd love to travel in this exquisite luxury, it doesn't say first class on our tickets so we may be in the wrong cabin," she shared, honestly. "We wouldn't want to take seats that have been booked by someone else."

"Oh dear," the hostess replied, as she looked at their passes. "You're right, it doesn't say first class at all. So... it's a good job *all* the seats are Firster Class then!" she giggled. "You see... This is a very special ML854. Modified to transport entire events, like the tournament. The bottom two decks are for storing cargo, and the top deck is for the passengers, and you can sit anywhere you like!" she explained.

"Anywhere we like, you say," said Zack.

Then suddenly, the boys shouted out in unison, with a "Window seat dibs!" from Fabio, and an "I bagsy window!" from Zack.

"Oh dear," said Dad. "If we all want to sit together then there's normally only one window seat. However do we decide who gets it?"

"Not a problem Sir," the hostess added, pointing further down the cabin "We have some table seats that have *two* window seats!"

"**AWESOME!**" howled Zack, and the boys dashed to claim their seats, while Mum and Dad stowed away their luggage.

"Oooh, look at all the buttons and gadgets on the seats," said Fabio. "There's something for everyone!"

"Dad, there's a recline button for you," said Zack.

"And heat and massage buttons for *you* Mum," said Fabio.

"And a built-in tablet with games and the internet for us!" the boys squealed.

"**AWESOME Times Two!**" cried Fabio, launching his arms in the air, then he ticked the 'boarding' check-box.

"Only one tick left now..."

After all the passengers were settled in their seats, the hostess ran through the flight procedures, and asked everyone to fasten their seatbelts, ready for... Takeoff!

14

JAY NINETY EIGHT

The double-quad engines roared into action with their high-velocity, high-pitched whirring, and the plane began to roll along the runway. As the jets got louder and **LOUDER!** The plane got faster and faster, and they left the ground with a deafening ***WHOOOOOSSSSSH***.

"Wooooo Hooooo!" cheered the boys.

Once the pilots reached their desired altitude, they levelled off the plane, and switched from double-quad engines, to just quad engines, and they cruised through the skies.

Fabio grabbed his clipboard, held aloft his pen, and put a huge tick in the final box. "There we go," he smiled. "We're officially on route now, and our

Emotional Rollercoaster is finally over... **NOTHING** can stop us now!" and for the next few minutes the boys fired up the tablets for some well deserved gaming time, Dad did some reclining, and Mum enjoyed some massaging.

"Hello," said the hostess, as she popped over to take their order for the mid-flight meal, and she quickly ran through all the options.

"And... all orders come with a side of our world famous, super-tasty, signature gourmet beans," she explained. "They're sooooo tasty, we've had passengers book flights just for the beans!"

"Mmm," sounded Mum and Dad, as they licked their lips, but Fabio and Zack were not so impressed.

"Thanks Miss, but no beans for us please," said the boys. "You see... we really, reeeaaaally, reeeeeaaaaally hate beans!" they added, as their faces contorted into maximum possible disgust, with tongues out, scrunched noses, furrowed eyebrows, and the biggest, bleurghiest, bleurgh sound they could make.

"Oh dear, well I can't possibly argue with that," said the hostess. "We want all passengers to have the best possible experience when they fly with us, so don't worry, I'll make certainly sure, with extra certainty, that not even a single bean touches your plates," she smiled.

"Thanks Miss," they replied, as the disgust faded from their faces.

The hostess keyed in their orders, making certainly sure, with extra certainty, to note 'NO BEANS!' for the boys, and then she whizzed off to take the other passengers' orders, who *all* wanted the beans!

"Hello my Champions," said Sixteen, as she stopped by to see how they were all doing.

"Hello!" they all replied.

"We heard all the cargo for the tournament is in the lower decks, is that true?" asked Zack.

"Everything but the venue," she replied. "All the consoles, computers, and arcades for the gamers, the lights and sound for the show, and even all the shopping stalls! We have BuilderDash merch, CataKarts merch, game exhibitions and demos, food kiosks, and even a cosplay store and a joke shop!" she explained. "If you like, I can take you all down there, and... you can pick a few things out!"

Fabio and Zack looked at Mum and Dad with

pleading eyes.

"Pleeeeeaaaaase," they begged, in their finest we-need-free-merch voices.

"Sounds like a fab idea," replied Mum and Dad, and they all ventured down to the middle deck.

"Now... I can't take you to the lower deck," Sixteen explained. "As that's where all the gaming machines are, and we're only revealing them on the day they'll be played."

"Oh, don't worry about these two peeking," Mum reassured. "They must be the most honest kids I know."

"Yeah," agreed Zack. "We're not like those sneaky cheater Jays!"

"Yeah," Fabio added. "I bet if *they* were on this plane, they'd be sneaking and peeking, like the sneaky peeking cheaty cheaters they are."

"Well, after all the sneaking and cheating they did in the last two tournaments, it certainly wouldn't surprise me," Sixteen agreed. "So lucky for us, there's no one called Jay on this flight," she confirmed. "Now... enough about those stinky cheating sneaky cheaters, we've got some awesome merch stalls to rummage through!" and they all scurried off to search.

Fabio bagged a BuilderDash bounty, Zack caught a CataKarts catch, Mum scored some Sixteen swag, and Dad picked a peculiar prank from the joke shop... A pot of... Tootin' Timmy's Rootin' Tootin' 'Splodin' Beans, with the 'splosive power of a thousand toots, packed into each and every one.

Sixteen shook her head at their meagre haul, then piled a few more bits on top. "There, that's a bit better," she smiled. "Now, are you okay making your own way upstairs, as our chat about those cheater Jays has left me a little paranoid, so I'm going to the lower deck to check there's been no pesky peeking at the games."

Mum, Dad, and the boys, thanked Sixteen for her generosity, then scurried up to their seats, to admire their treats, as Sixteen ventured down to the bottom deck.

She crept silently down the final step, and peered into the distance of the vast, dimly lit, cargo bay, where the hulking forms of shrouded arcades were concealed beneath dark heavy tarps. They lined the sides of the deck, leaving just a narrow pathway between, and the only sound was the muffled whirring of the engines.

As she continued quietly down the aisle, she

suddenly spotted a contorted shadow skulking in the distance, hunched over and creeping from one machine to the next, sneaking and peeking under each cover.

Sixteen's chrome suit began glowing orange as her heart rate increased, and she advanced towards the shadow.

The light startled the crooked figure, and it suddenly twisted, staring directly at her, before vanishing into the cargo.

Sixteen dashed over, her armour now pulsing red with anger, and thrust her arm into the darkness. She seized the sneaking shadow, and dragged it from its hiding place.

"**GOT YOU!** you sneaking cheater. **WHAT ON EARTH** are you doing?" she growled. "The knowledge of these gaming machines is highly hush-hush, confidentially-classified, super-secret information, that's literally under wraps... under heavy tarp wraps to be exact! **WHAT** are you doing down here!" she barked again.

"Sorry Sixteen, sorry madam," the cowering figure whimpered. "I'm a new caterer; I was just... erm... looking for the gourmet beans for supper service. I didn't see anything, I promise. I don't even know anything about gaming," she snivelled.

"Oh my goodness," Sixteen gasped, straightening the young lady up, and dusting her off. "I'm the one that should be apologising. Our last few tournaments have been plagued by a growing cheater group that call themselves the JAYs, so I'm becoming increasingly paranoid and protective of our secrets," she explained. "I'm terribly sorry for startling you; you'll find the gourmet beans, with all the other stock, on the middle deck."

"Thank you madam, thank you Sixteen, I'm so sorry, I'll never come down here again, I promise," she apologised some more, as she scuttled off.

"Please, no apologies necessary young lady," Sixteen called out to her, before she left. "Oh, and what's your name my dear?"

"It's Jayne madam," she replied innocently, as she glanced back, then dipped her head and continued scurrying away... "JAY-N-E," she muttered under her breath with a sinister snigger... "JAY-Ninety-Eight..."

15

ROOTIN' TOOTIN' 'SPLODIN' BEANS

J ayne scampered up the stairs to the middle deck, grabbed a box of gourmet beans, which she clearly knew the location of, and was about to make her way back to the kitchen when she passed the cargo for the joke stall and suddenly stopped.

"Hmmm," she paused. "Yes... these will do nicely," she cackled. "These will do veeeeery nicely," and she snatched a few pots of Tootin' Timmy's Rootin' Tootin' 'Splodin' Beans, then scurried to the kitchen.

Jayne passed the gourmet beans to the busy chefs, who were preparing the mid-flight meals, then snuck off to read the label on the joke beans:

WARNING!

These beans contain extreme Tootin' power!

Directions: Add one single bean to each portion of normal beans, then sit back and howl with laughter when the Rootin' Tootin' Toot-time begins.

The gourmet beans were being served in proper-posh petite porcelain pots, called ramekins, so Jayne swiped three empty ones, filled them with the joke beans, and sneakily warmed them up in the microwave, before taking her place at the service counter, so she could intercept every plate that left the kitchen.

Jayne's evil plan for the three toot-powered servings was to put a full portion on both Fabio and Zack's plates, insanely more than the one bean recommendation, and then... to prevent too much attention to the tootin' boys, she would drop a single bean into all the other orders, from the third serving.

As the orders were called, Jayne carried out her despicable plan, placing bean after bean, until finally... the orders for Fabio and Zack's table were up...

Jayne rubbed her hands together with glee and

placed the parp-powered pots, neatly on their plates.

"Service!" she called out, quietly sniggering under her breath.

The hostess whisked away the plates, added them to her sparkling silver service trolley, and gracefully glided out of the kitchen, but when she saw the plates for Fabio and Zack she screeched to a halt.

"Oh dear... that won't do at all," she muttered to herself, shaking her head. "Those adorable boys clearly explained how much they hated beans, so I'm not going to spoil their flight by serving them even a sniff of one," she continued. "But I'm certainly not wasting these little pots of gourmet joy, so which lucky person is going to get them?" she pondered, tapping her chin.

She quickly checked the other orders on her trolley, and found the perfect one! One of the pilots, nicknamed Jett, just happened to be her best friend, and she also happened to... **LOVE** the gourmet beans! So she added the two spare pots to Jett's plate, then began serving the meals.

When she got to the room behind the cockpit, she knocked on the door, excited to see Jett's expression at the extra servings, but the co-pilot answered instead, nicknamed Wings.

Now Wings loved the gourmet beans just as much as Jett. In fact, if at all possible, he loved them even more! But unfortunately for them, the pilots were never allowed to eat the same meal, so in the ultra-rare case that something was wrong with the food, both pilots wouldn't fall ill.

To keep things fair though, Wings and Jett made a gourmet bean-binding pact agreement, where they take turns to order the beans, and this flight was Jett's turn.

Wings took the plates from the hostess, and his eyes bulged out of their sockets when he saw Jett's triple serving, but then all the excitement drained from his face when he spotted his beanless meal.

"Heeey, why don't I ever get triple pots when it's my turn to have beans," he complained.

"Sorry Wings. I know how much you both love them, but we had a couple spare and I didn't want to waste them," she explained.

"I understand," grumbled Wings. "We can't let these tasty tubs go to waste, but please promise the next spares come to me, when it's my bean turn."

"I promise," smiled the hostess, and she glided off to finish serving the meals.

Wings closed the door and was just about to take the plates through to the cockpit when a little voice popped into his head... his Naughty Wings voice...

"Oh Wingsy," it said. "You *could* be a nice man and take all three pots to Jett, but *she* doesn't love them as much as you do, so why don't *you*... eat two!"

Then a different voice popped into his head, this must be his Nice Wings voice, coming to the rescue...

"Oh Mr Wings..." it said. "Don't listen to Naughty Wings; you'll just get into trouble, as the hostess and Jett are besties. No... what you need to do is... Execute the Triple Bean Sneak, and sneak a sneaky fork full from each serving! You'll get your share of the beans, without moving a single pot!"

You see... concerning gourmet beans, Wings didn't have a Nice Wings voice to come to the rescue at all.

"What's taking so long with our meals?" barked Jett. "I need my beans!" she demanded.

"On my way now," Wings hollered back, from the room behind the cockpit.

He quickly snuck a sneaky fork full from the first pot, flipped over a Yorkshire pudding, and stashed it underneath. Then he loaded up another fork from the second pot, lifted the lid of his pie, and hid it in there. And for the final fork load from the third pot, he dug a little hole in his mashed potato, and buried them inside (a never before seen bean sneak, that even Mum would have been proud of), and he smiled with sneaky satisfaction as his Triple Bean Sneak was complete.

He served Jett her meal, who was delighted to see three pots, but then slightly confused that they only looked half full, then he turned his back and tucked into his hidden hordes...

Shortly after everyone on the plane had finished supper, the Tootin' Timmy's bean tally was at: zero for Fabio and Zack, the passengers had consumed a single thousand-toot-powered bean each, but... the pilot, and co-pilot, had wolfed down roughly an entire pot each! That's more tootin' power than a super-sized stadium, packed with a super-sized vuvuzela-tootin' crowd, and the effects were starting to kick in...

At   first,   the   passengers   looked   a   little

uncomfortable, with rubbing of rumbling bellies, bodies wriggling in chairs, flustered faces reddening with embarrassment, and a few dashed off to the bathroom for a sneaky private toot. But soon all the toilets were full... and they could fight their gaseous urge no more...

16

THE TUNE OF A
THOUSAND TOOTS

The performance, or parp-formance, to describe it more accurately, began with the release of a single long-lasting **tremendous** toot, and its signature sound of a beautiful brass trumpet, which echoed its way down the cabin.

The passengers looked around nervously, with the classic *'it wasn't me'* look on their faces, but then soon began laughing, which gave them the confidence to relieve *their* rumbles, with the release of their very own Roaring Rippers... and **The Tune of a Thousand Toots** commenced.

Zack quickly leaped up, grabbed a chopstick from an empty plate, and took his centre-aisle stage as the conductor of this wondrous wind-powered orchestra.

There were farts from the front, and squeaks from
the sides, as Zack waved his arms, to keep them in time.
There were wind-breaking whooshes,
and a nose-pinching pong, as the musicians
played on, with their gaseous song.

Ear-piercing whistlers, had the cabin in stitches,
Paint-peeling parps got them cackling like witches,
The low-booming blasts, got plenty of laughs,
As the tooting continued, in the opera of gas.

Zack sped up the tempo with
poofs, pongs and poppers,
And whoopees and whiffers and
whirl-windy whoppers,
And screechers and stinkers and
stenchy seat shakers,
And blats, blurts, and blurpers,
and bold breezy breakers.

Then Zack raised his arms, for the concluding cloud,
And a big burly man, rose up from the crowd,

He glanced up and down, the air-busting craft,

And began to prepare, his grand-final draft,

He let out his finest, harmonious vent,

His air bomb of thunder, a shockwave it sent,

But who was this man, this famous kaboomer,

This man was renowned, as the

world famous tooter,

A triumphant trumper, from the day he was born,

His name and his title, the Flatulent Foghorn.

After Foghorn's final fart, there was a moment of silence... Then, the entire cabin erupted with cheers and applause, as they gave themselves a standing ovation at their fantastic farting feat.

They didn't quite understand what had just happened, or even how it happened, but they had so much fun that they didn't really care! In fact, they decided their parp-formance was sooooo awesome, that they needed an equally awesome band name, and quickly settled on **Flatulent Foghorn and the Fuselage Foggers!**

The laughter and fun continued in the cabin, but the situation in the cockpit was much more dire. The pilots had wolfed down significantly more joke beans than everyone else, and had become quite unwell. They were doubled over with stomach pain, unable to leave their private bathrooms, and therefore... unable to **fly the plane!!!**

It was currently cruising on auto pilot, with a single air hostess, panicked and distressed, as she explained the situation to Air Traffic Control.

With the pilots out of commission, no one was checking the dashboard instruments, or the flight-path weather, and they coasted straight into a terrifying torrential thunderstorm, causing a sudden violent shudder to the plane.

Back in the cabin, the passengers were initially startled, but then all agreed it was just a lingering jolt from the air-bomb-of-thunder's shockwave. But... when the seatbelt lights came on, and the cabin crew rushed in, concern swept across their faces, and worrying whispers could be heard all around.

The staff tried to ease the passengers and explained that the plane had drifted into a thunderstorm, so they should expect some mild to moderate turbulence, which seemed to work, as everyone calmly returned to their seats, and clipped in their belts.

The crew then asked if there was a doctor on board, which startled the passengers again, proving a bit more difficult to calm, but luckily, the gaming tournament had a full complement of staff which included a small team of paramedics, who instantly jumped up and offered their services.

The hostess failed to mention that the aid was for the pilots, as she hoped a doctor could get them back on their feet, and after a few tests, and providing some basic medication, the paramedics advised that the pilots will make a full recovery! But... not for at least another twenty-four hours! The hostess would need to find someone that can fly and land the plane.

As they continued rattling through the storm, a knee-shaking hostess nervously entered the cabin to address the concerned commuters, and when she admitted that the pilots were ill, and unable to fly the plane, their concern levelled up to... Panicked Passengers, and they were getting louder and more agitated.

"I, I understand this is troubling news," she stuttered. "But please understand we're doing everything we can to rectify the situation, and please also note that this plane is fitted with state of the art technology, and advanced auto-pilot and auto-land features, but... I **will** need your attention for one last question..." and the crowd all glared at her, granting a brief moment of silence... "Just in case of an emergency... we have to have someone at the controls, sooo... does anyone onboard know how tooooo... fly a plane?"

17

BLITHERING BABBLE

The question from the hostess was the final straw for the patrons, and the cabin erupted with ranting and raving and shouting and wailing and countless arms flailing, as they quickly descended into an unruly mob.

But amongst all the chaos, two little hands rose up into the air, and two little voices cried "We can!" But their words went unheard, drowned out from the uproar.

The boys stretched their arms as high as they could go, with Mum and Dad joining in too, and shouted again "**We can!**" But it was still no match for the rioting rabble... until one person noticed their efforts.

"**SILENCE MORTALS!!!**" the voice roared. It was Sixteen of course, and she shot up from her seat, her suit pounding with its intense red glare, and her powerful voice reverberated through the plane. The cranky commuters went completely quiet, leaving just the background sounds of the whirring engines, the howling storm, and creaking metal, as it battered the plane.

"While *you're* all busy complaining, instead of thinking of ways to support, your **blithering babble** is drowning out the only two people actually offering to help."

"Well *I* don't see anyone," a voice mocked from the crowd.

Sixteen rushed over to Fabio and Zack, "Come on my heroes, stand and be seen," she said.

Initially, they were a little nervous about the reaction from the grumpy group, but they knew they could help so they proudly rose up from their seats.

When the passengers saw it was Fabio and Zack, the grumbles, mumbles, and all other 'umbles, returned.

"*Kids???*" one voice shouted.

"We know you're great gamers but **this isn't a game!**" another called out.

"Yeah, this is real life, and I'm not putting mine in

the hands of a couple of **children!**" a third complained.

"**SILENCE!!!**" came another shout, but this time it wasn't Sixteen... it was Mum, and she bolted up from her seat to defend them. "**Yes, Kids!**" she replied to the first. "The same *'kids'* that have conquered flying challenges that even the best pilots in the world have failed at," she challenged the second. "And I'd trust my life in their hands, over any of **yours!**" she concluded to the third, pointing angrily across the crowd.

"**And my life too!**" echoed Dad, jumping up in support.

"**Don't forget mine!**" Sixteen added.

"**And mine!**" the hostess yelled from the front. "And I can confidently confirm that these boys have indeed out-flown the best-of-the-best on Wicked Wings. Their run went viral across all the airports and not a single pilot could match them. Fabio and Zack... it would be my absolute honour to escort you to the cockpit, and I'm certainly certain that ground control would agree," she proudly praised.

"**SO!**" Sixteen called out. "**Anyone think they can do better?**" but all the commuters went silent. "Come on, don't be shy, anyone think they can fly better than my champions?" but they all just looked down into their laps, trying to avoid eye contact. "**Ha, No... I didn't think so!** Come on boys, I do believe you have a plane to land," and Mum, Dad, Sixteen, and the boys, followed the hostess to the cockpit.

As the door to the flight deck opened, they were instantly hit with warning sounds beeping, caution lights blinking, and a terrifying view of the fierce storm battering the windshield, as the plane hurtled through the dark thick clouds.

The hostess at the controls was still distressed, and now in tears, desperate for someone to take over, as the auto pilot struggled to navigate the storm. When she saw that help had arrived, she cast off her headset and dashed over to hug them all.

"Thank you, thank you, thank you so much" she wept.

They all glanced across the cockpit, and its endless sea of complicated controls, and the grown-ups let out a gasp. But the boys just looked at each other and smiled, as it was almost identical to the Wicked Wings simulator.

A flash of lightning in the distance, and a dip of the wings, knocked them all off balance. It was their urgent cue that time was against them.

Fabio clambered into the pilot's seat, Zack into the co-pilot's seat, and they put on their headsets with a serious glare.

Mum, Dad, and Sixteen, stayed for support but remained in the background and completely silent as not to distract them, and the cabin crew left to attend to the passengers.

"Fabio and Zack reporting for duty," they said, in their finest military tone.

"Hi boys, it's great to hear your voices," replied the main controller. "I'm Skye, and my team and I will be with you every step of the way," she reassured them. "When we received the distress call, we checked the passenger list for anyone with flight experience, and when we saw your names, smiles and relief swept across everyone here in Air Traffic Control. We know this is a very challenging challenge, but we've all seen your impressive viral performance on Wicked Wings, so we're delighted you answered the call for help," she explained. "And finally... don't worry about using all that formal pilot chatter, as no one else will be using this channel."

"It's our pleasure Miss," the boys replied,

"And just to let you know Miss," added Zack. "We *LOVE* challenging challenges!"

"And that amazing attitude is exactly why you're the perfect pilots for the job," Skye agreed. "Now, do you need us to direct you, or do you already have a plan?"

"Well, all these warning lights and alarms are *really* annoying us Miss, so our first plan is to deal with *them*," Fabio replied, but as they were checking the dials and screens, a sudden blinding flash, deafening rumble of thunder, and a gale-force blast of wind, shook the plane violently, causing more blinking bulbs and sirens.

"Are you okay there boys?" asked Skye. "We saw that weather spike on our monitors."

"We're fine Miss, but now there are *even more* annoying alarms blaring!" replied Zack. "I've scanned all the instruments and have some good news and bad news, which would you like first?"

"Erm, the bad news first please Zack," said Skye.

"Ok, well looking at the weather data and read-outs, the auto-pilot and auto-land computers cannot safely navigate this storm, and the plane is becoming increasingly unstable."

"You're right Zack, we were just about to say the same, you'll need to stabilise the plane," agreed Skye. "So, what's the good news then?"

"Well... it just so happens, we have our very *own* flight computer that can navigate even the most impossibly-impossible storms, and his name is... **Fabio!**" Zack beamed. "So I say we disable these dangerous automatic controls, and switch to manual," and he glanced over to Fabio for his approval, who nodded back in agreement, with a steely glare.

Skye knew it was the only safe option, so she instantly authorised the deactivation of the auto pilot. "Are you ready Fabio?" she asked.

Remembering the force from the Wicked Wings machine, Fabio grabbed the controls so tightly that his fingers went white, and he pushed his feet firmly on the pedals, "I'm ready Miss."

"Okay then, on your count Zack," said Skye.

Zack got ready at the switch, "**Three... Two... One...**" *Click...*

18

AAAAAAAAAAAAA!!!

The plane shuddered violently as the autopilot disabled, and the force transferred straight through to Fabio, who struggled to keep control. He pushed all his weight onto the yoke, for additional support, and his arms trembled as he wrestled against the wicked weather.

As the battle continued, Fabio began to understand the storm, countering its breezy blasts, and after a frantically furious fight, he managed to stabilize the plane.

The emergency lights and blaring alarms gradually ceased, and before long, they were cruising steadily through the storm.

"**YES!!!**" they all cheered.

"Fabio, that was amazing!" Skye praised. "How did

you steady the plane so quickly?"

"Well..." he began. "This is going to sound a bit strange, but the storm is... erm... talking to me."

"Talking?" replied a baffled Skye. "But... but... how?

"I'm guessing from my years of gaming," Fabio explained. "I appear to have built up lightning fast and super sensitive reactions, so I can instantly respond to all the information on the screen, and this is no different. The storm is sending that exact same information through the force in the flight controls, so all I need to do is understand them and react."

"You make it sound so easy," said Skye.

"I think he's being a teeny tiny bit modest there Miss," added Zack. "It's much more amazing than that. You see... Fabio was born with an amazing brain of amazingness, and can calculate seemingly impossible things, that most of us don't even understand. He makes it sound easy, because for him... it is."

"Wow, that *is* amazing!" said Skye.

Just then a hostess rushed in, "Are we through the storm, are we through the storm?" she cried out in excitement. "The passengers felt the plane stabilize and they're all cheering in relief."

"I'm afraid we're still in the storm Miss," Zack replied, pointing at the horrendous conditions through the windscreen. "And looking at the weather readings, things are going to get much worse as we're about to hit a hurricane!" he warned. "Fabio and I **will** get everyone through this, but for now, please tell the passengers to hold on tight... as it's about to get real rocky."

"Will do Sir," the hostess saluted, before she rushed off to prepare everyone.

"Great job spotting the hurricane Zack," said Skye. "Unfortunately there's no way to avoid it, as the auto pilot kindly flew you straight into the middle of a... triple hurricane storm! And it's not long before you need to land!"

"We'll need another plan then!" cried Fabio, still grappling with the gnarly gusts.

"**Got one!**" Zack called out, after quickly scanning all the possible flight paths. "We can't escape above or below the hurricane yet, so the safest route is to go through... the... huge dangerous one right in front of us!"

"Erm, Zack... wouldn't the safest route be the smallest, least dangerous one?" Fabio queried.

"I'm afraid the huge dangerous one, *is* the least dangerous!" he replied. "The second option is a huger, we-lost-a-couple-of-engines dangerous, and the third option is the hugest, where-have-the-wings-gone dangerous!"

"I see," said Fabio. "Then... the huge dangerous one it is!"

"Well done Zack! How did you manage to find that so fast?" asked Skye. "It would probably take us ten times as long, and about ten times as many people, to work through all those possible flight paths."

"I found it quite similar to searching through the internet," replied Zack. "And I'm quite good at that."

"Now who's being modest," said Fabio. "It's actually much more amazing than that. You see... Zack, or Earl Findington of Scrollville, also has an amazing brain of amazingness, and he's the master of the internet! He can find anything in the blink of an eye, even seemingly impossible things."

"Wow, that's amazing too!" said Skye, "So basically... **You're both amazing!**"

"Thanks Miss," they both replied.

"Right, back to the plan," said Zack. "So... I plot the

safest route, patch it through to you both, then brief the crew, and finally, inform the rest of the plane through the intercom. And, as soon as we hit the hurricane, I'll provide non-stop real-time navigation to Fabio, just like when I'm the navigator in our favourite rally-car game."

"Sounds like a great plan Zack!" said Skye. "Actually, scrap that, it's better than that, it's... **The Perfect Plan!**"

Fabio and Zack looked at each other with ultimate determination on their faces, and nodded, "**Let's do this!**"

Zack plotted a rough path through the first part of the hurricane, sent it to Fabio and Skye's screens, and explained that he will fine tune it when they're actually in it. He then briefed the crew through the private channel on the intercom, then prepared his poshest voice as he activated the speakers in the cabin.

"Good evening passengers, this is your co-pilot speaking. As you are aware, we have managed to stabilize the plane by switching to manual controls, after the auto pilot kindly flew us directly into a triple hurricane. Our only escape is to fly through the smallest of the three, so apologies, but the ride is going to get a bit bumpy, and maybe a little bit scary too. The staff have been briefed and will guide you through all the safety procedures, but please... **do not worry!** We have flown this exact route hundreds of times, in much more horrendous conditions, and no matter what challenges are ahead of us, we promise to get you all safely through this. Zack out."

The cabin crew were expecting another rebellion, but the passengers took the news quite well. They appeared to have a new-found respect for the boys, and they followed all the orders from the staff.

Back in the flight deck, everyone strapped in tight, and Zack counted down to impact.

"Three... two... one... BRACE!" and as they hit the hurricane, they were blasted with even harsher winds, which howled harrowingly across the plane.

The steering column was shaking uncontrollably from the force, and Fabio was struggling to cope.

"Zack help!" he cried. "I need to keep both hands, on the yoke, and I don't have a third hand to control the engines or thrust.

"*I'll* be your third and fourth hands," said Zack. "Now, **CLIMB!**" he shouted, and he flipped a switch for another engine which roared fiercely into action.

The plane was now thundering through the storm on five of its eight engines, and the increased speed and immense power of the plane, helped Fabio fight the storm.

"**Thhaannkkss Zaacckk!**" Fabio stuttered, as his body and voice trembled from the vibrating controls.

Zack saw another violent blast approaching on the readings. "**CLIMB!**" he yelled again, throttling up, and Fabio glided over the gnarly gust.

An area of intense lightning was right ahead, "**DIVE!**" Zack called out, throttling down, and they plummeted beneath it, watching as jagged lines of dazzling neon pink, streaked just above them.

Their close friendship made them an unstoppable force, as they worked together in perfect harmony, almost as if they could read each other's minds.

"Okay," said Zack. "We're approaching the eye wall, the most dangerous part of the hurricane, with the insanest of wind speeds, spiralling up and up. If we try to fly against it, it could rip the plane apart, so we'll have to spiral up with it... Ready?"

"**Ready!**" Fabio replied, with unwavering focus.

"**Three**... **two**... **one**... **CLIMB!**" shouted Zack, firing up the sixth engine, and Fabio pulled back on the controls, soaring up into the dark swirling clouds of the eye wall.

Their speed and angle were slightly off, putting tremendous force on the wings, which began wildly wobbling. The boys needed more power... FAST!

"**THRUST!**" Fabio called out, and he tilted the plane to realign it, as Zack engaged the seventh engine, providing another almighty boost.

They fought to match the surging spirals of the storm, and eventually removed the pressure on the plane, allowing the wings to steady.

As they coasted along the inner eye wall, riding it like a surfer through the barrel of a wave, the vast expanse of the hurricane eye became visible. Its eerie calmness exposed the black sea beneath, and the twinkling stars above, surrounded by a turbulent vortex of grey swirling clouds.

"**Fabio!** We need to break away from the wall, and down into the descending air of the eye," ordered Zack. "Then fly to the other side, and ride it up and out of the storm. If we can nail this manoeuvre, we can escape the hurricane!"

"Ready when you are," Fabio called out, as he prepared himself.

"**DIVE!**" howled Zack, sharply reducing thrust, and Fabio plunged them down into the eye.

They quickly levelled off the plane and cruised across the cloudless centre, towards the whirling wall of wind on the opposite side.

"**CLIMB!**" Zack cried out, as he activated the final engine and throttled up to maximum thrust. Fabio pulled the yoke, leaning back with all his body weight for additional force, and they began to climb the inner eye wall, racing furiously against the speeding spirals of air."

"**Aaaaaaaaaaaaa!**" they shrieked, as all eight engines blasted them through the menacing mist, driving them higher and higher, the force rattling the plane and everything in it, the deafening din of the storm hurling every last bolt, rumble, and gust, it had at them, the clouds reaching out like ghostly arms, lined with veins of blinding blue lightning, and twisted fingers of frightening fog, snatching at them, one, after another, after another, trying desperately to drag them back...

until suddenly...

19

THE CRAFTY CUNNING CYCLONE

The harrowing noise from the storm ceased, the blinding flashes faded, the clouds parted, and the violent rattling forces retreated... The boys had boldly battled in the battle of all battles, and they had finally escaped... They had thwarted the typhoon, vanquished the vortex, and conquered the cyclone... They were the heroes of the hurricane.

Zack throttled down to cruise and powered down four of the engines, as Fabio levelled off the plane, and they glided through the calm clear sky, above the wild wicked weather below.

But things were not quiet for long...

Everyone in the cockpit, Skye and her team through the headsets, and all the passengers and cabin crew, cheered an enormous resounding "**YEEEEEEEEEEEEESSSSS!!!!!**"

Well, all but two people that is... Wings and Jett were far too unwell to be cheering, but they were still contributing to the celebratory sounds with their own enormous resounding noises from their non-stop tooting!

With the entire plane still cheering, Zack clicked on the autopilot, turned to Fabio, and held out his arm. Fabio let go of the controls, his fingers numb from the vibrations, locked hands with Zack, and gave a firm winning shake. They had no words worthy of congratulating each other on their mammoth achievement, so they just looked at one another and shared a single, sharp, nod of accomplishment.

Mum and Dad looked over at their brave boys and their eyes began to well up. They were desperate to congratulate them with the hugest hug they could find in their hug-for-every-occasion catalogue, but they were unsure if it was safe yet.

The cheering was too loud for the boys to be heard so

Fabio mouthed the words "It's okay," and Zack gestured for them to come over.

Mum and Dad unclipped their belts and rushed over to embrace their boys, with tears streaming down their faces.

"Fabio, Zack," they cried. "You cannot possibly imagine how proud we are," and they hugged them tightly.

"You made it boys!" Skye crackled through the comms. "The autopilot should be able to finish the flight and landing without a hitch, and I know we've asked so much of you already, but please could you stay in the pilots' seats, just to keep all our minds at ease?" she asked.

"It would be our absolute pleasure Miss," they replied.

"Putting the terrifying typhoon of torment aside," added Zack, "Being able to fly a real plane has been a dream come true Miss."

"Well from your performance today, I'm sure you'll have every airline and flight school on the planet, desperately trying to recruit you!" Skye praised. "Now, back to business… The autopilot has been updated with all the latest storm information, so once it has passed the hurricane, it will begin its descent for landing. All you have to do is sit back, relax, and enjoy the ride." And just as she had explained, the autopilot continued on above the storm, and out of harm's way, and as soon as they passed the final furious grey swirling arm, the plane began its descent.

With the hurricane finally behind them, there was nothing more to worry about, but... the Crafty, Cunning Cyclone was not finished with them yet...

While the celebrations continued, with music booming, and lots of chattering, smiling, hugging, laughing, dancing, and the classic clinking of glasses, the innocent partying patrons were completely oblivious to the sly sneaky storm, and its sneaky scheming plans, and it fired out its fierce final attack...

A thick bolt of blinding light crackled as it streaked across the evening sky, and hammered straight into the plane with a deafening strike, followed by a thunderous rumble, instantly knocking out the power, and casting everyone into complete darkness.

Fabio called out to Skye through the comms, but there was no response, the comms were out. Zack tried to alert the passengers, but the intercom was down. Fabio flicked the autopilot on and off, but it was completely disengaged. The only light in the cockpit was a scattering of faint glowing emergency buttons, but worse than all that... The engines were out!

Fabio grabbed the yoke and managed to level the plane, using only manual and mechanical controls, but without the engines, the plane was descending, so once again, they had to act FAST!

"**Mum! Dad! Strap in!**" ordered the boys, and in the darkness, they felt their way back to their seats, behind Fabio and Zack's, and secured their belts.

"We need someone to get a message to the passenger cabin quick! Does anyone have a light?" asked Zack.

"**I will be the light!**" a strong voice responded, and Sixteen stood up tall, her suit pulsing, and illuminating the space around her with a warm amber glow.

"Perfect," said Zack. "Tell everyone to strap in and remain calm, everything is going to be okay, I have a plan."

"Yes Sir!" she saluted, and she dashed off to alert

everyone.

Fabio and Zack could barely see each other, but that didn't faze them, they just thought back to the Wicked Wings machine and knew exactly what to do. There was no time for panic, no time for Double-Sweat Danger, and certainly no time for Triple-Sweat Terror.

Zack flipped up the cover for the reboot button and pounded it with a clenched fist. A few clicks could be heard, then the lights flickered, and then the engines tried to spin up, but then... everything shut down again.

"**It's overloading!**" Zack yelled. "There's too much trying to reboot at once," so he quickly disabled every system but the main computer, and hit the reboot button again, and after a few more clicks, the CPU booted up. "One down... many more to go," he called out, then began testing each module, and every possible combination, until...

"Critical flight systems, back online Fabio!" he cheered. "But I'm afraid the autopilot module is fried... We're going to have to do this the old fashioned way and land this thing ourselves."

Zack quickly diverted his attention to the engine

switches and toggled them all on, but they kept failing and were not powering up properly... The lightning strike must have damaged them too.

"Erm... Fabio?" Zack probed.

"Yeeeees," he replied, trying to manually align the plane to the airport, while still in descent.

"How many engines do you need to land this monster?"

"Well... believe it or not Zack... I got so good at my flight sim games that I tried a more difficult challenge... landing with the engines turned off!" he explained. "So I guess that means I don't need any! But... I think everyone would be a bit more comfortable if we had at least two."

"Of course I believe it Fabio! I was the one who suggested it remember, after you S-ranked every route you tried... on your first attempt!" said Zack. "Anyway... I'm on it," and he began testing them one at a time.

Click...

Click...

Click...

"Engines one, two and three are completely gone I'm afraid Fabio." He then clicked on the fourth and it began spinning up, with its high pitched metallic whining, sending a wave of relief across everyone in the plane.

"We have thrust!" exclaimed Zack, pushing the throttle forward, and Fabio began the landing procedure.

"We need comms now Zack, so we can communicate with Skye and the airport," Fabio requested. "And lights would be nice, if they're not fried too!"

"They're next on the list buddy!" and Zack booted up the communication panels and enabled the lights, which flickered a few times in protest before giving in and staying on.

"Fabio, Zack, do you read me?" Skye's voice crackled through the headset. "We completely lost you, is everything okay?"

"Just about," Fabio replied. "The sneaky scheming storm had prepared a final parting gift for us, and struck us with a blinding bolt of lightning, knocking out every electrical device on the plane."

"Oh my goodness," Skye gasped. "How did you fix it?"

"Zack did everything!" Fabio beamed. "He tried every reboot combination until he found one that worked and managed to get all major systems online, and... one engine!"

Click, click, click... CLICK... WHIRRRRR "**YES!!!**" yelled Zack. "Make that two engines!"

"Zack, that's amazing!" cheered Skye. "That's all the auto-pilot and auto-land modules need, for a safe touchdown."

"Ahhh, about those..." added Zack. "They went kaput when the storm dealt its final blow. We're on the good ol' fashioned mechanical controls now."

"Okay, well no computer could achieve what I know you boys are capable of, so no pressure... but I'm expecting the smoothest landing in aviation history," Skye joked. "But if you need any help bringing her in, just holler. I've opened a private emergency channel with the airport too, so we can all communicate together."

"Evening Fabio and Zack, this is control tower alpha here," a male voice buzzed through the headset. "My name's Mac and I'm here to help if you need me."

"Hi Mac," the boys replied. "Are you up to date with our status?" added Zack.

"Sure am, and it's great to finally hear your voices," He replied. "Skye filled me in on all the details, and I just caught the last bit now. As you're aware from your Wicked Wings performance, this airport is a little on the, erm... little side, and you're piloting a plane that's a little on the, erm... big side. But don't worry! We have you on radar, you're looking great! and... **you're cleared for landing!**"

"Thanks Mac, we're on approach now," Fabio advised.

Just as before, Fabio and Zack were working together in perfect harmony, with Fabio's flawless flying, and Zack's precision on the throttle, slowing as they approached.

As soon as they were within range, Zack called out "Gear Down!" and he grabbed the lever for the landing gear, shoved it down, and waited for them to lower, but... nothing happened...

He tried again, and muttered a much more stern "**Gear... DOWN!**" But still no movement...

20

EMERGENCY BUTTON

I t was clear that the lightning had also damaged the electrical motors, that raise and lower the wheels, but it wasn't something they could have tested mid flight, as lowering them during cruise could damage them.

Fabio's head slowly turned to face Zack…

"Zaaaaack?" he probed, nervously.

"Yes Fabio," Zack calmly replied.

"Where's our landing gear, and why aren't you panicking?" Fabio fretted.

"Is everything okay boys?" Skye and Mac called through the comms.

"All good here!" Zack responded confidently.

"But Zaaaaack! We can't land without the landing gear! Why are you being so calm?" Fabio fretted some more.

"Because, my best friend Fabio... This is the one area where not being a perfect pilot, finally pays off... You see..." He began, as he reached below the central console and pulled out a big red emergency button, revealing a crank. "When I first started playing flight sims, I wasn't instantly flawless, like you, I had many occasions where parts of the plane may have gotten, shall we say... a teeny, tiny, teensy bit damaged." An understatement, so far under the statement that it's gone through the earth, past the core, and is now on the other side of the planet! "So... I quickly learned all the reboots, resets, and manual overrides for every possible pesky pickle I got myself into," he continued, turning the crank. "This is probably one of the few parts of a plane that you had no idea even existed Fabio, as you've never had to use it, but *this* is the Gravity Release, or the Zack-Messed-Up-Again Crank, as I like to call it. It's saved my flight-sim bacon countless times," he explained. "Now... when you hear the click, get ready for a bit of drag as the wheels will extend down using gravity, no fried motors required." he concluded, and sure enough, there was a click, and Fabio felt the change in drag through the controls.

Fabio and Zack focused all their attention on the narrow runway, making the precision adjustments needed to squeeze the mammoth liner onto the tiny toothpick of tarmac, which was barely wide enough to even fit the wheels! Imagine an elephant trying to tightrope walk.

With the landing gear fully extended, they were on track for a perfect arrival. The hurricane was now just a distant memory, but its final feeble remnants were still trying to nudge the plane with weak wisps of wind, but their pitiful pats of pressure were easily dusted off by Fabio and Zack, and the mighty MegaLiner.

The boys kept the plane solidly straight, and as the wheels softly met the runway, they finally touched down, and the plane began to slow.

The wings whooshed gently past the miniature control tower below, and Mum, Dad, Sixteen, and the boys got ready to celebrate, when suddenly... the door to the flight deck burst open, and a panicked hostess rushed in, panting.

"**Quick! Strap in quick!** We're about to experience some severe turbulence!" she squealed.

"Turbulence?" queried the boys. "But we've almost stopped."

But sure enough, as the plane slowed to a standstill, it began shaking and shuddering. Then the ground began trembling and the noisy blaring sirens returned. Then they saw bright blue flashes, and red lights flickering, and then... the wind began blasting down onto the plane.

"**AAAAARRRRRGGGGGHHHHH!!!!!**" screamed Fabio.

"**AAAAARRRRRGGGGGHHHHH!!!!!**" shrieked Zack.

Then they looked at each other for one final, double-powered "**AAAAARRRRRGGGGGHHHHH!!!!! THE HURRICANE MUST BE BACK!!!!!**"

"Oh no, it's nothing like that," said a much calmer hostess.

"Then why is the plane shaking?" asked Fabio.

"Oh, that's just the passengers jumping around, celebrating," she replied. "That's what I rushed in to warn you about."

"I see..." said Fabio.

"Okay then... What about the sirens, the trembling ground, and the lightning flashes?" Zack pressed further.

"Oh all that, yes I spotted that through the windows on my way here, that's just from all the big, heavy, emergency vehicles rushing in, just in case anything was wrong... Look," and she pointed to the ground outside.

"Hmmm, yes, I see that... now..." said Zack.

"Alright then..." Fabio continued. "What about all the wind blasting down onto the plane? That *must* be from the hurricane."

This time the hostess didn't have an answer, and she looked equally puzzled.

"Oh that," Mac buzzed through the comms. "That's just the helicopters from all the news stations," he explained.

"Helicopters!" howled the boys. "Ahhh yes, they must be for Sixteen and the gaming tournament," Fabio innocently added. "Sixteen is *very* famous, and there's so much hype about the competition, that... of course all the news stations will want an interview."

Mum, Dad, and Sixteen all looked at each other and smiled.

"Come on my dearest boys, this has been a truly

unforgettable adventure, and a non-stop emotional rollercoaster, but I think it's time we departed now," said Mum, opening her arms.

"Just one last sec," they replied, and they switched on the comms channel for the passenger cabin.

"Attention passengers, this is your captains speaking. It brings us the greatest of pleasures to announce that we've arrived safely at our destination. Thank you for flying with us. Fabio and Zack out."

The rumbling from the cabin suddenly intensified and loud cheering could be heard all around.

Fabio and Zack unclipped their harnesses and got up to leave. They glanced back at the cockpit one last time and gave the console a gentle pat.

"Well done plane," they whispered under their breath. "We did it!"

A huge mobile stairway was driven to the exit door of the plane, and once all the passengers and staff had left, Mum, Dad, Sixteen, and the boys, stood at the door and looked down.

The crew and commuters were lined up at the bottom of the stairs, followed by a huge crowd of reporters, emergency personnel, and fans. Further back, was a semi-circle backdrop of fire engines, police cars, and ambulances, all flashing away, and a scattering of Media vans from the newspapers, television, and radio. There were even a few army trucks, and people and vehicles were still arriving.

"*Sixteeeeen?*" Fabio asked with a querying tone.

"Yes, my little champion," she replied.

"That's quite a lot of people out there... Could *you* go first please?" he asked. "I get a bit nervous with crowds."

"Of course my dear," she replied, and proudly led them down the stairs, followed by Zack, holding hands with Dad, then Fabio, clinging tightly to Mum's arm, and they were all met with cheering, applauding, whistling, whooping, and all the other 'ings that adoring crowds do, bundled with camera flashes from every angle, including from the helicopters above!

As they strolled through the passenger-lined aisle, everyone shook hands with the boys, and offered their deepest thanks. Even the poorly parping pilots were there to thank the boys in person.

Sixteen continued on towards the crowd, and all the reporters rushed forward with their cameras rolling, and a fuzzy sea of huge fluffy microphones on long skinny poles.

"Wow!" said Fabio and Zack to one and other. "She's even more famous than I thought!"

But then something completely unexpected happened...

21

SALUTING HANDSHAKE OF ONE-KNEED BOWINGNESS

The reporters didn't stop when they got to Sixteen... They ran straight past her, and straight over to the boys! But... before they even had a chance to ask any questions, the crowd suddenly parted and a huge shiny-black super-stretched limousine pulled up before them.

"Wow! I wonder who *this* could be," said Fabio. "That car looks very important so it must be a VIP."

"Hmmm, it looks even more important than that to me, so it must be a VVIP, or even... a VVVIP!" added Zack.

Two men in smart black suits rushed around to open the car doors and, to the shock and amazement of everyone... one of the highest ranking officials stepped out, and began marching towards them, followed closely behind by his security and entourage.

The boys suddenly began fretting as they had never met someone so official before, and they didn't have the slightest of foggiest of clues, how to greet one.

"Quick! What do we do," Fabio whispered to Zack "Do we bow, do we kneel?"

"Maybe," Zack whispered back. "Or do we salute, or just shake hands?"

"I don't know Zack, and he's nearly here! This is more stressful than flying the plane!"

The VVVIP was now standing before them, and they were in such a manic muddle they ended up doing a mega-mix meeting mash-up, and greeted him with a Saluting Handshake of One-Kneed Bowingness!

But the VVVIP began shaking his head; he did not appear to be very happy with their greeting.

"No, **no**, *no*, NO, no... this will not do at all, young men," he objected, shaking his head some more. "You boys do not do the Saluting Handshake of One-Kneed Bowingness for us..." and he looked around at the entire crowd and nodded his head...

"*WE*... do the Saluting Handshake of One-Kneed Bowingness... for *YOU!!!*" his booming voice bellowed, and then he, his entourage, all the passengers, the staff, and then the entire crowd... saluted, knelt, bowed, and reached out their hands to Fabio and Zack.

The VVVIP then opened a small brown wooden case and awarded them with a medal of bravery, but he was struggling to find a perfect place to pin it.

"Please, allow me Sir," came a familiar voice from behind. "I think I have just the thing you need," and Mac strolled up with two pilot's blazers.

"Hang on a minute... We know that voice... *Maaaaac!!!*" yelled Fabio and Zack.

"Hello boys, these are from our young cadets club, they should be just about the right fit, and you've more than earned them," and he helped them into the blazers.

"Thanks Mac!" they replied, as their eyes lit up with excitement.

"Yes, that's perfect, thank you Mac," said the VVVIP, and he attached the medals to their jackets.

"Thank you Sir!" they said with a salute, as their excitement levelled-up to ecstatic.

The VVVIP personally thanked them for their bravery, and amazing accomplishment, and went along with them to chat to the reporters and pose for a few photos.

Mum and Dad watched with pride as Fabio and Zack mingled with the crowd.

"Look at our boys," said Dad, with a sniffle. "They're growing up so fast."

"I know," Mum agreed. "Too fast if you ask me... I'm not sure I'm ready for them to grow up just yet," she added, wiping a tear from her eye.

Just then, the boys looked back at Mum and Dad, almost as if they knew, and they ran over to them as fast as they could, crashing into them and burying their heads into their tummies, with the hugest hug they had!

You see... the boys had a hug-for-every-occasion catalogue in their minds too, and Mum and Dad were in desperate need of a huge dose of the WSYLB... The We're-Still-Your-Little-Boys hug.

Just then, another helicopter flew overhead, much bigger than the news ones, and it landed a little further up the runway.

A lady got out and began running to the boys. She had a white shirt with gold and black insignias on her shoulders.

"Oh my goodness, I'm so glad I caught you. We flew over as soon as we could as I wanted to personally thank you before you left," she explained, panting from the sprint, and she knelt down to them and offered them a formal pilot's greeting.

"Hang on a minute... we know that voice... *Skyyyyye!!!*" they screamed.

"Now... don't worry about using all that formal pilot stuff Miss," they said, and they wrapped their arms around her and squeezed her tightly. "Thank you for being there for us Skye."

"And thank you for being there for us too," she replied. "Now let me take a look at you both in your smart new cadet blazers," she said, as she took a step back to admire them. "Wow, you look amazing and I can see our VVVIP has awarded you with a well deserved medal of bravery, but... there's just one thing missing," and she pulled out two shiny badges and attached them just above the medal... Their very own training wings!

Fabio and Zack had now reached their maximum-level of excitement, any more and their heads may explode!!!

"And providing your parents are okay with this," Skye continued. "We have two places waiting for you at our flight school!" and she handed them both a letter.

"That's it!" they said. "We cannot take any more... **Danger! Danger! Excitement Overload!**" and they made an explosion sound, with all the actions, then pretended to do a very dramatic, and completely over-the-top faint.

"Fabio... Zack... wake up!" said Mum, playing along. "Oh dear, their brains must have exploded from all that excitement, look they're not moving at all."

As they continued their performance, trying desperately not to move, with their blinking eyelids and grinning mouths totally giving them away, they heard another voice... a different voice... a girl's voice...

"Fabiooo... Zaaack... please wake up," she said adorably.

The boys snuck a sliver of an eye open to see who it was, but as soon as Zack realised, his eyelids peeled back, he sprang up straight, and his heart started pounding fiercely, like nothing he had ever felt before...

"Elle!" he cried, wrapping his arms around her, unable to contain his emotions, and a tear rolled down his cheek. "How?"

"You and Fabio are all over the news you know, so we came as soon as we could," she explained, pointing through the crowd, to her parents waiting at their car. "I can't believe you've gone through all this, just for me and my little old Yiayia," and a tear rolled down her cheek too.

The reality had hit Zack hard. The journey, the medals, the blazers, the wings, the flight school... It was all very exciting and incredibly rewarding but it wasn't the reason they came... They came for Elle and her grandma.

"Well we did, Elle, this is all for you both, and we haven't even got started yet, have we Fabio."

"Nope," Fabio replied, getting up and introducing himself, and they all nattered away for a bit, like the nattering natterers they were, with Elle's parents coming over to join in the nattering too!"

"Right then gang!" exclaimed Zack. "That's another

challenge completed, and just part one of our amazing gaming journey, what's next on the list Fabio?"

"Oh nothing much…" he replied. "Just the… most ultimate five-day gaming tournament in all gaming history."

Fabio, Zack, and Elle all looked at each other with a steely glare and nodded…

"Challenge accepted…"

To be continued…

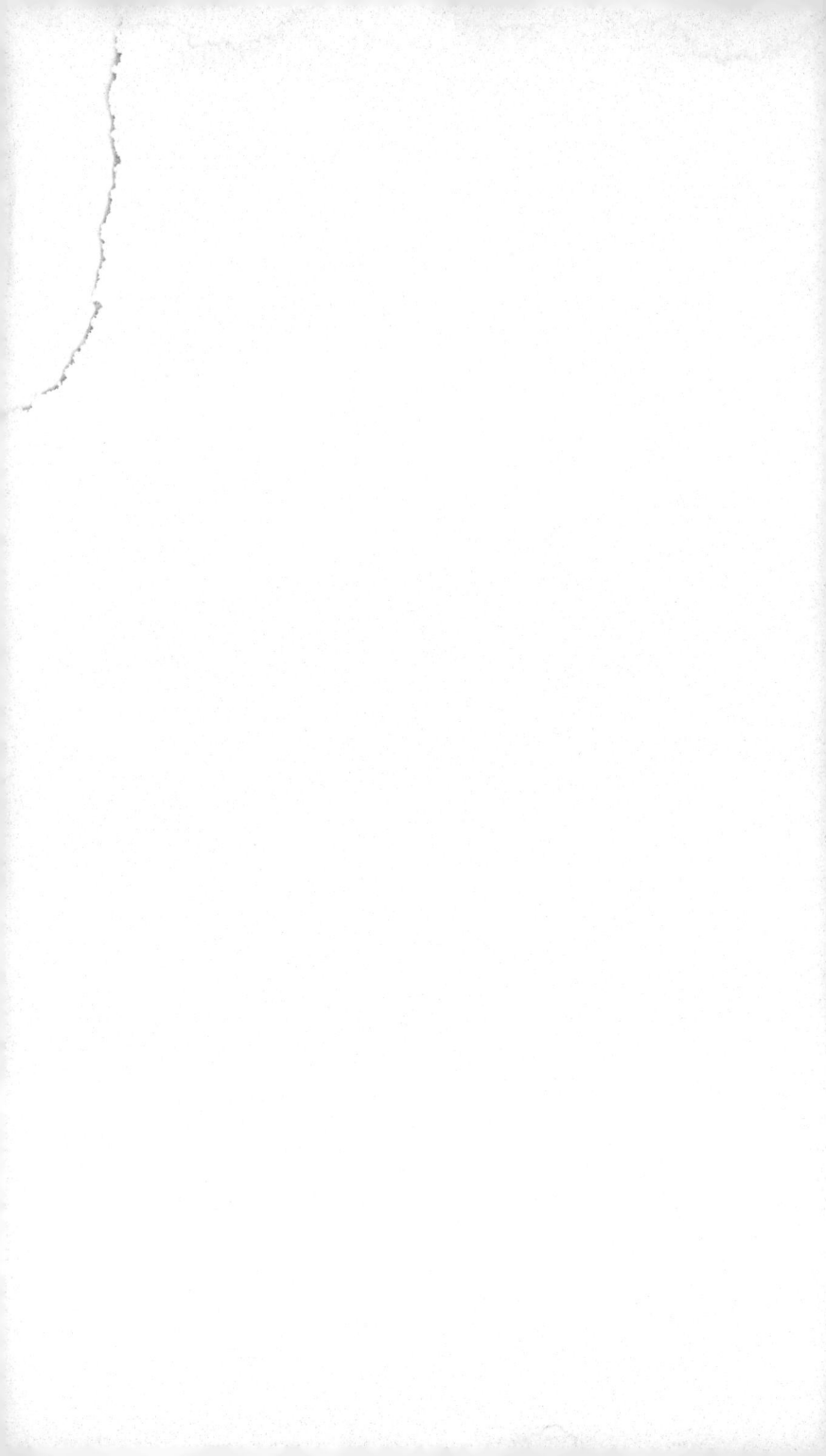

Printed in Dunstable, United Kingdom

64491578R00109